California Lobster Diving

Biology
Gear Selection & Rigging
Regulations
Techniques
Cooking & Eating
Where to Hunt

by
Kristine and Steve Barsky

D0034345

Hammerhead Press
Santa Barbara, California
www.hammerheadpress.com

Original photography and illustrations by Steven M. Barsky. Additional photography and illustrations by John C. Black, Skip Dunham, Mark Conlin, Bob Evans, the California Department of Fish and Game, NiteRider Technical Lighting Systems, Ed Stetson, John Suchil, and Nancy Vander Velde.

Printing History
First Edition, 2000.

Printed in the United States by Ojai Printing and Publishing Ojai, California

International Standard Book Number
ISBN: 0-9674305-2-6

Library of Congress Catalog Card Number: 00-103136
Barsky, Kristine and Steve
California Lobster Diving

Other books by Kristine and Steve Barsky

Published by Best Publishing
Careers in Diving
 – by Steven Barsky, Kristine Barsky, and Ronnie Damico
Small Boat Diving – by Steven M. Barsky
Spearfishing for Skin and Scuba Divers – by Steven M. Barsky
The Simple Guide to Rebreather Diving
 – by Steven M. Barsky, Mark Thurlow, & Mike Ward
The Simple Guide to Snorkeling Fun – by Steven M. Barsky

Published by Scuba Schools International
The Dry Suit Diving Manual – by Steven M. Barsky

Published by Team Vision, Inc.
Diving with the Divator MK II Full-Face Mask
 by Steven M. Barsky
Diving with the EXO-26® Full Face Mask – by Steven M. Barsky

Published by Hammerhead Press
Dry Suit Diving, 3rd Edition – by Steven M. Barsky
Diving in High-Risk Environments, 3rd Edition
 by Steven M. Barsky

WARNING!

WARNING: Scuba diving is an adventure sport which always involves some degree of risk of personal injury or death. When you engage in lobster diving you add additional risks which include entanglement, overweighting, out-of-air emergencies, fatigue, and entrapment. Many people who engage in lobster diving have put aside their good judgement and placed themselves in situations that have led to their deaths. This has occurred with divers who have gone into caves, removed their tanks to enter small holes, and failed to adjust their buoyancy after collecting a bag full of lobsters.

The authors remind you that there is no substitute for proper training in diving techniques, conservative judgement, proper gear maintenance, and regular participation in diving. Every dive always places the diver at risk of personal injury and death. It is up to the individual to minimize these risks and know when it is better not to dive or when it is time to get out of the water. Only you can make these decisions for yourself. If you choose to exceed your own limitations, or the limitations of your equipment or training when you dive, you must be prepared to accept the responsibility for any consequences that may occur.

Acknowledgements

Our best ideas for books have always come from our friends and this project was no exception. First and foremost we would like to thank Michael Zolkoski of Pacific Books/Shoreline Press for his idea to do this book. It was his recommendation that got us started and we are especially grateful to him for his thoughts and suggestions for marketing and ways to improve our publishing business.

Shane Anderson is the marine collector at UCSB and one of the most knowledgeable people we know when it comes to the marine creatures of the Santa Barbara coast. Shane was a valuable consultant on this project for his knowledge of lobster habits and the local environment. He also took the time to proofread the book.

Don Barthelmess at Santa Barbara City College provided us with access to their training tanks for shooting the photo of Kristine with the giant lobster. Without the crane in the diving department there we would not have been able to handle a lobster of that size and keep it under control.

John C. Black allowed us to use his great photo of Ed Stetson and Curt Wiessner.

Our mentor and friend Bob Christensen contributed to this book in innumerable ways, both directly and indirectly. He has helped us to grow, and our lives are much richer because of our relationship with him. Bob is an outstanding diver and a constant source of thoughtful advice.

Photographer Mark Conlin provided the great photos of the moray eel and the sea otter for the chapter on lobster biology. Mark is an outstanding cameraman whose work has appeared in numerous books and magazines.

Many thanks to the kind ladies of Coastal Catch in Santa Barbara who assisted us with our photography. Nancy Lovegreen and Jody Gerhart's assistance was invaluable and their enthusiasm about everything is contagious.

Diving instructor Bill Lidyoff let us in on some of his favorite diving spots and gave us insights to diving in the Laguna Beach area. Bill has always been available to help us no matter what type of project we have in progress.

John Duffy, Assistant Executive Director of the California Fish and

Game Commission, not only critiqued the manuscript, but also let us in on many of his secret lobster spots.

Dive partner and friend Skip Dunham has always shared his techniques with us, as well as his secret dive spots. Many of our best underwater adventures have been with Skip, who is one of the top lobster divers in Santa Barbara. Skip provided several of the photos for the book and also took the time to proofread the manuscript.

Jane Dunham, Skip's wife, is also a dear friend and the most gracious hostess we know. Her recipe for lobster cocktail is one of the best you'll find!

Mark Perlstein, longtime diver, friend, and avid underwater hunter also reviewed the manuscript and recommended many improvements. Mark's underwater experience spans many years and his insights into lobster diving were extremely helpful. Mark also shared some of his favorite lobster spots with us.

NiteRider Technical Lighting Systems allowed us to use a photo of one of their outstanding head mounted lights. These systems are extremely popular with night divers. Their equipment is top quality.

Joan Robinson at Ojai Printing and Publishing has been a constant source of technical information and assistance in our work. We could not have done this project without Joan's assistance and the help of everyone at Ojai Printing.

John Suchil, Fish and Game lieutenant, allowed us to use several of his photographs taken in the field aboard the patrol vessel, *Yellowtail.*

Artist Nancy Vander Velde produced the excellent lobster illustration used to show the different parts of the lobster's body. Nancy's work is outstanding and has regularly appeared in magazines like *California Diving News* as well as many other projects.

Warden Mike Ferrence of the California Department of Fish and Game took the time to pose for photos aboard the P/V *Yellowtail.* The work of the wardens is essential to preserving our marine life and enforcing the Fish and Game laws.

Without the assistance of these kind people we could never have finished this book. Thanks to all of you!

Steve and Kristine Barsky
Santa Barbara, California

Table of Contents

Table of Contents

CHAPTER 1
GET READY TO GRAB LOBSTERS!

Of all the diving activities in California, diving for lobsters probably involves more people than any other. The excitement that builds as opening day of lobster season approaches is like no other time during the year. Old tanks get hydrostatically tested, private boats are tuned up, and game bags and lights are purchased in mass quantities. The dive charter boats are usually booked by dive stores and clubs several years in advance and getting a space on opening day can sometimes be impossible.

It's not just that people like to eat lobsters; it's that catching them is fun and exciting, too. Lobsters respond to people in ways that no other creature equals. It's not unusual for a lobster to come part way out of its hole to check you out, making some beginners think that

Kristine Barsky herds a big one back to the corral!

catching lobsters is easy. However, lobsters move so fast it takes most new divers a season or two before they begin to catch lobsters on a regular basis.

People do wild things to get lobsters, things they probably would not normally do if they were thinking straight and not half-crazed by the sight of an eight pound lobster staring at them from back inside a hole. We've seen more than one diver take off his tank and push it ahead of him or let it float behind him in order to wiggle back into a tight hole. When you think about it, behavior like this is a bit mad, given that you can buy a lobster at the market usually for much less than what it costs to go on a dive boat for a day!

Aboard the dive boats, one of the most exciting moments is when everyone returns from a successful dive and spills their catch onto the deck. The lobsters snap their tails back and forth and their legs scratch the deck. There's always a slight undercurrent of competition to see who has the most lobsters or who has the biggest one.

Be sure to take pictures of your lobster with you in your dive gear aboard the boat. To make your lobster look bigger hold it away from your body, close to the camera. Everybody loves to see photos of divers with big lobsters!

Half the fun of lobster diving is in reliving the adventure at the end of the day as you sit around the table with family and friends enjoying a meal of boiled or grilled lobster. You get to show off the cuts in your hands where the lobster's spines pierced your gloves and the sea urchin spines stuck under your skin when you got careless making your grab. With a little melted butter, a salad, some french bread, a glass of wine or a beer, nothing is tastier than a meal of freshly caught lobsters.

Non-divers can legally catch lobsters by using hoop-nets, but that form of "fishing" is not widely practiced. We think that diving for lobsters is much more fun!

California lobster diving is more challenging than lobster diving in many other locations because California lobsters can only be taken by divers by hand. You can't legally use a spear, snare, net, hook, or any other device. Only your gloved hands are allowed. If you miss a lobster on your first grab and the hole is deeper than your arm is long, you probably aren't going to get a second chance at that lobster that day.

Lobsters are considered exotic fare, and for this reason, many people never get the opportunity to enjoy them. As a diver in southern California, you have an opportunity to catch and eat lobsters from October through the middle of March, or five and a half months out of each year.

We recommend that you read this entire book, including the chapter about the biology of lobsters. The more you know about their lifestyle and habits the more effective you will be at finding and catching lobsters. In addition, each chapter is filled with hints, tricks, and tips that will make you a more efficient hunter. Read this book carefully and you'll be well on your way to successful California lobster diving!

Get Ready to Grab Lobsters!

Dee Dee Barthelmess and her father Don get up close and personal with the giant bug, "Lobzilla."

Chapter 2
The Biology of the
California Spiny Lobster

Good hunters know their prey. Whether you're catching lobsters, taking photographs of them, or just want to observe them in the wild, you've got to know where they live, as well as their habits, to find them successfully. In this chapter you'll learn the secrets of the lobster's life that will help make you a better lobster diver.

How Lobsters are Classified by Scientists

Scientific names and classifications can be intimidating at first, but helpful once you understand the logic behind the system. The method of classification is a hierarchy that gets more specific as you progress.

The spiny lobster is a member of the animal kingdom. The next division in the classification scheme is called the phylum and lobsters belong to the phylum Arthropoda, which translates from the Latin as "jointed feet." Arthropods are an invertebrate group, which means they lack a backbone or spine. All of the insects also belong to this phylum, and it's no coincidence that lobsters resemble their land based cousins or that divers commonly refer to lobsters as "bugs."

The "class" is the next segment in the scientific classification, and lobsters belong to the class known as "Crustaceans," which means "hard shelled." They have their skeleton on the outside of their body, which makes it impossible for them to grow unless they shed their shell.

As we get more specific in our scientific classification, the next group is the "order." The four major "families" of lobster in the world all belong to the order known as the "Decapoda" (or ten-legged).

The family Palinuridae is where we separate the spiny lobsters from the more well known American lobster or clawed lobster from the East Coast. The family Palinuridae contains only animals that look like spiny lobsters. The genus name is *Panulirus*. There are over a dozen species of this genus worldwide that are all very similar, and are all found in relatively warm water (if you consider California water "warm").

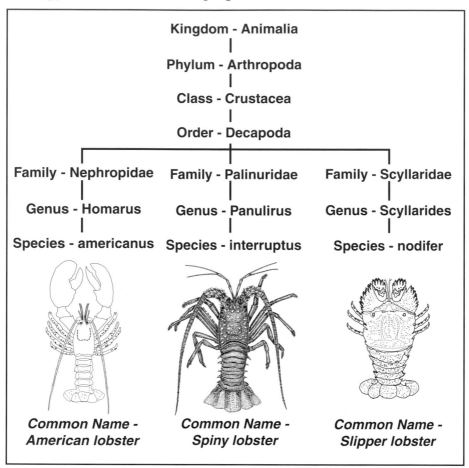

Kingdom - Animalia

Phylum - Arthropoda

Class - Crustacea

Order - Decapoda

Family - Nephropidae	Family - Palinuridae	Family - Scyllaridae
Genus - Homarus	Genus - Panulirus	Genus - Scyllarides
Species - americanus	Species - interruptus	Species - nodifer

Common Name -
American lobster

Common Name -
Spiny lobster

Common Name -
Slipper lobster

Classification of the California Spiny Lobster.

To be completely precise we refer to an animal by its unique "genus species" name. The California spiny lobster's scientific name is *Panulirus interruptus*, and a scientist anywhere in the world would know exactly which type of spiny lobster you were talking about. The brick red one, with black and yellow eye spots, and grooves in each tail segment that don't go all the way across, but are "interrupted," that lives in rocky reefs and crevices from Point Arguello to the northern portion of Baja, Mexico. You can't get more specific than this!

The Range of the Spiny Lobster

When you read about the California spiny lobster in the scientific literature, the range is usually reported as Manzanillo, Mexico to Monterey, California. However, the majority of the population occurs between Magdalena Bay in Baja California (Mexico) northward to Pt.

The range of the California Spiny Lobster is from Magdalena Bay in Mexico to Monterey.

Conception, including all the offshore islands in southern California. An isolated population is also reported on the northwestern shore of the Gulf of California. Small numbers of spiny lobsters are sometimes found as far north as the Monterey peninsula.

Should you be diving in the Gulf of California you could encounter *Panulirus inflatus*, the "langosta" or blue spiny lobster whose northern range overlaps that of *P. interruptus*. *P. inflatus* has bold, regularly spaced spots and blue antennae. The two species don't mate with each other, which is one of the main reasons they are considered different species.

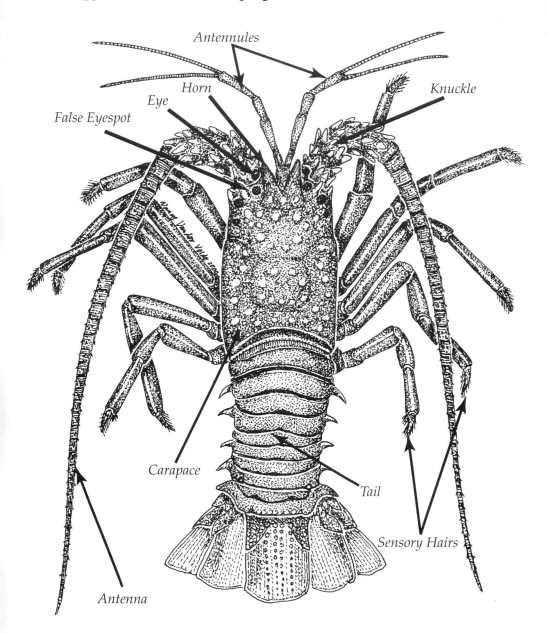

Antennules

Horn

Eye

Knuckle

False Eyespot

Carapace

Tail

Sensory Hairs

Antenna

The anatomy of the California spiny lobster is similar to other spiny lobsters.

Lobsters Have a Unique Body Structure

The spiny lobster's body or exoskeleton has two main parts: a carapace and a tail (or abdomen). The tail is segmented and there are swimmerets or "pleopods" under each segment. Females have larger and broader swimmerets than males. The female's eggs are carried on the swimmerets until they hatch. When the tail fan is extended it has five segments.

The spiny lobster's ten legs are jointed, and the black tips have sensory bristles on them. The hair-like receptors on their legs respond to a range of chemicals, temperature, and touch. California spiny lobster can detect increases and decreases in temperature of one and a half degrees Fahrenheit or less.

Spiny lobsters have a pair of heavy, spiny antennae that are longer than their body. Generally they are held out in front of their body and track any movement like radar. Lobsters use their antennae to monitor predators so they can keep a safe distance away. Lobsters also have a pair of short, double-ended antennules between the larger antennae that they use for "smelling" food and predators.

The body of the spiny lobster ranges from brick red to a reddish brown. The bright orange coloration of lobsters seen in the market is due to cooking. Two eyespots or false eyes are located above the antennules. Your eye is immediately drawn to the eyespots due to their bright gold coloration and not the true small stalked eyes above them.

The compound eyes of the lobster are like those of an insect, and can detect the slightest movement. However, adult lobsters don't like bright light. Some scientists suggest that their eyes are adapted to their dimly lit environment, and out of water it is suspected they are almost blind.

Their Best Offense is a Good Defense

Lobsters generally move by simply walking forwards, backwards or sideways. They do all equally well. They can move rapidly on their legs, but usually climb slowly around and over rocks in search of food. An escape technique utilized when a more serious threat is at hand, is rapid backward swimming. This is done with quick flaps of the muscular tail, and is very disconcerting if you're not expecting it. The antennae trail behind as they swim, and the legs are drawn up beneath the body making the lobster very streamlined.

Although they are capable of delivering powerful tail thrusts, the lobster quickly tires. Consequently the backward swimming is done in short bursts, and usually can't be maintained for any distance.

Of course, for every rule, there is the exception. We've heard of one story where a diver came across a large bug on a sandy bottom off Palos Verdes. Thinking that this would be an easy catch, the diver made two "casual" grabs at the lobster and missed both times. The first time the lobster jetted back a few feet. Following the second attempt, the lobster took off for the surface, 50 feet away. Although the diver tried to follow as quickly as he could, he couldn't keep up with the lobster and watched it break the surface, take a few more strokes there, and jet back down to the bottom. As the lobster headed back for the bottom, it seemed to the diver that it actually accelerated away! The moral of this story is that you must be aggressive when chasing lobsters, because in most cases, they will not stick around to give you another chance...

Because they lack the large claws of their East Coast cousin some people call the spiny lobster a "crayfish," which is a common mistake. You'll also hear some people insist that they can taste the difference between East Coast lobsters and spiny lobsters. While the claw meat has a different texture and flavor than the tail meat, the tails of both species taste so similar that only a true gourmet might be able to tell the difference.

For their defense, spiny lobsters have numerous spines on their carapace, their antennae, and on the edge of each tail segment, which can inflict painful injuries to the unwary diver. The two largest spines on the lobster's body are over their stalked eyes, and are frequently referred to as "horns."

Gloves should always be worn when handling spiny lobsters because any of the spines can puncture your water-softened hands. One flex of its powerful tail and your fingers or palm can be sliced open.

Like many crustaceans, spiny lobsters are capable of "autotomy." That means they can break off their legs or antennae if they are being held by a predator. They have a special joint mechanism that rapidly seals with a membrane where the break occurs. This prevents blood and body fluid loss. Many a successful escape is frequently made with just the loss of a leg, however, there is a price to pay. The energy that would normally be directed to growth and reproduction is now funneled into regeneration of the missing limb(s).

Divers should never deliberately grab or pull on a lobster's legs. A lobster that loses more than three legs might escape, but probably will not recover from its injuries.

Autotomy also can assist a lobster with a difficult "molt," the process where the lobster sheds its shell to grow. If the lobster can't pull a leg free it can break off the limb rather then remain trapped half in and out of its molt. If a lobster expends too much energy during the molt, it will die of exhaustion before it recovers enough to feed again. Lobsters cannot repair punctures or breaks in their carapace! If a spear point or a tooth breaks the carapace, the lobster will eventually die.

Lobsters are dined upon by a variety of fishes and other creatures.

Sea otters will feed voraciously on lobsters, when they have the opportunity.

Although moray eels and lobsters are frequently found in the same hole, the lobster can become a victim of the moray when it molts.

They are food for giant sea bass, kelp or calico bass, California sheephead, California scorpionfish or sculpins, rockfishes, cabezon, horn sharks, and leopard sharks. Small lobsters also fall victim to larger lobsters.

Lobsters are also a favorite meal for the two-spotted octopus, sea otters, and California moray eels. We know you're going to say that

Sheephead love lobster. We've watched a large sheephead inhale the antenna of a captured lobster as we held it prior to bagging!

you've found moray eels and lobsters in the same hole. That's true, but it's a tenuous relationship. When the time comes for the lobster to molt, you can be sure it will not be sharing a hole with a moray or a larger lobster.

If you hear an alarming grating noise, it is a warning sound produced by a structure at the base of the lobster's antennae. Scientists refer to it as the "stridulatory organ." We personally have heard a lobster "stridulate" after being thrust into a pot of boiling water.

Sex and the Single Lobster

California spiny lobster sex is unusual, brief, and not very romantic. A male lobster will approach a female and, when given the opportunity, will straddle and cradle the female to deposit the sperm packet on her "belly." They approach each other and when they get close, they stand as high as possible on their hind legs. The male swings the female underneath him so they are belly to belly. The sperm are in a gelatinous mixture, which the male extrudes through a readily visible opening at the base of the last pair of walking legs, in a putty-like packet called a "spermatophore."

The word "plastered" is slang for a female that has had a spermatophore attached to her belly. When the spermatophore is first extruded it's a light gray color. After it hardens it turns a dark gray-black. Some divers think it looks like a wad of chewing gum, but there's no mistaking what it is. The term "tarred" is another expression divers use when referring to a female with a spermatophore.

Female lobsters have much larger "swimmerets" than male lobsters.

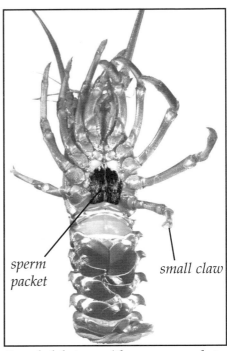

Female lobsters with a sperm packet attached to them are said to be "plastered."

This female lobster is carrying eggs. Note that the sperm packet which was present in the photo above right is now gone.

Biology of the California Spiny Lobster

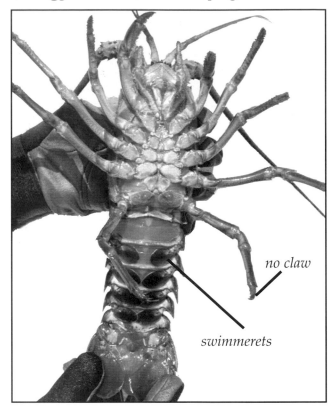

Male lobsters have smaller swimmerets, and lack claws on their last pair of walking legs.

no claw

swimmerets

Female spiny lobsters have small claws on their last (fifth) walking leg on each side. When the female is ready to release her eggs, through a tiny opening at the base of each third pair of legs, she reaches down with her clawed legs and scratches the sperm packet open. The sperm then fertilize the majority of the eggs as they are released and attached to the underside of her swimmerets. Only fertilized eggs will success- fully attach.

Mating takes place between January and April. Female lobsters usually move into shallow water at the end of March or early April and release and fertilize their eggs in May and June. The eggs are usu- ally a bright coral red when they're first produced. When they hatch ten weeks later, they're usually a dark brown color.

When the young hatch, they begin life as a creature known as a "phyllosoma larvae." Looking at the illustration of the phyllosoma, you won't be surprised to learn it took scientists many years to realize that this open ocean drifter was actually the first life stage of the lob- ster. Phyllosomes have long, thin appendages that allow them to move agilely as they drift along. They are serious predators on other plank- tonic plants and animals drifting with them. The phyllosoma larva has to undergo 12 molts before it changes into a new creature known as a "puerulus larva." This takes roughly 6 to 9 months.

A great number of the phyllosoma become meals for other marine inhabitants during this period. Consequently, a female lobster usually produces large numbers of eggs. The number of eggs produced is usually proportional to the lobster's size. Ninety percent of the females are usually sexually mature (ready to produce eggs) at a carapace length of 2.7 inches. A first time mother will produce over 100,000 eggs, while a female with a carapace length of over six inches will produce close to a million.

If the phyllosoma survives to complete its twelfth molt, a puerulus larva emerges. The puerulus (meaning child) looks like a miniature adult with extremely long antennae. It is transparent and the tiny swimmerets on its tail propel the larva into shore. The puerulus does not feed, and its goal is to take the lobster to suitable habitat nearshore. If suitable habitat is located the puerulus sinks to the bottom and after a few days molts into a juvenile lobster.

Juvenile spiny lobsters flourish in warm, food abundant areas found particularly in surf grass beds. These beds also provide lots of hiding places for the young lobsters. The loss of nursery habitat directly impacts the survival of this species. Not only juvenile lobsters like this habitat. Many divers successfully hunt lobsters in the shallow waters of surf grass beds. Areas with the greatest surf grass (*Phyllospadix spp.*) abundance produce the most lobsters.

Spiny lobsters grow in rapid spurts by shedding their entire shell or exoskeleton. This process is known as "molting." Lobsters usually

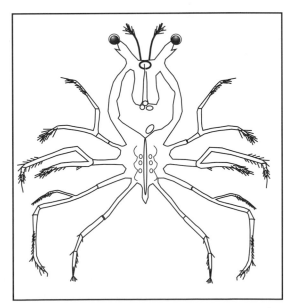

Phyollosoma are produced in large numbers because few survive to become adult lobsters.

molt in August through October, right after they complete the reproductive cycle.

Before the lobster sheds its shell, a new, soft-shell forms underneath its existing shell. Molting is a stressful and dangerous time for the lobster. They lose their appetite and usually try to find a safe place to hole up. It usually takes more than one molt to completely regenerate a lost limb, so if you see a lobster with a miniature appendage you know it's a survivor of some sort of an attack.

Molting takes place extremely rapidly, but before they molt lobsters must first form an entirely new shell under the existing one. This new shell has the texture of latex rubber. Prior to the molt, the lobster must also withdraw calcium from the old shell so they will be able to harden the new one. This action also softens the old shell, making molting easier. They store the calcium in their blood in anticipation of the molt.

At night, when molting usually occurs, the new, slightly smaller lobster emerges from its old carapace through a split on the dorsal (back) surface between the carapace and the tail. If all goes well, it quickly pulls its legs and antennae free.

While the new shell is still soft the lobster literally stretches it by

This molt might look like a live lobster at first glance, but look at the gap between the carapace and the tail. Also, note how the tail is offset from the carapace.

How big is this bug? This 14 pound monster was taken by Skip Dunham of Santa Barbara.

pumping water into its cells. During this time, the lobster will have to wait for the new shell to harden before it can assume its normal activities. When its shell is soft, it offers little protection from hungry predators. The calcium stored in their blood from the old shell is used to harden the new one.

Lobsters molt frequently during their first year of life. During the second year the animal usually molts four times and may have attained a carapace length of 2 inches. The number of molts continues to decline until they reach only one a year. An animal that has lost appendages or not fed well might not even molt annually. Large lobsters do not molt every year.

Studies have yielded different rates of growth for lobsters depending on the location and most likely, the diet of the animals. It is safe to say that it can take 5 to 7 years for a lobster to reach sexual maturity, and sometimes years longer to reach legal size.

It's fun to imagine how big a spiny lobster can grow. There have been reports of animals reaching 25-30 pounds! The lobster in the picture on page 17 is roughly 14 pounds. Males usually grow larger than females. Since lobsters shed their exoskeleton to grow, there's no way to measure their age. Estimates vary from 50 to 150 years of age.

Sport divers have always sought trophy animals. Consequently, the stocks of old, large lobsters have mostly disappeared. Animals over 10 pounds are now uncommon. A growing number of conservation minded divers have brought these large animals back to the boat, had their pictures taken, and released them back into the wild.

Lobsters are Scavengers

Spiny lobsters are not finicky eaters. They are efficient predators and scavengers. They'll eat snails, sea urchins, clams, sponges, kelp, worms, mussels, scallops, barnacles, fish and even other lobsters. The California spiny lobster is an important predator on the purple and red sea urchin.

The California spiny lobster has a serious set of jaws that is capable of breaking up shells and bones. We suggest not probing the mouth parts of a lobster with anything you value!

An undersize lobster that was being held at a Department of Fish and Game office was fed some whole little neck clams. It would pick up a clam with its mouth parts and press it into its jaws. A loud crack could be heard as it shattered the shell and picked out the clam meat!

Being a nocturnal animal, lobsters forage and dine at night.

Consequently, you're more likely to encounter them out in the open after dark. They normally hunt individually when they're searching for food. However, during the day, they hole up in crevices and holes with other lobsters. When they get older, the males especially, will become solitary except during breeding season.

Lobsters Move Throughout the Year

Over the course of a year, California spiny lobsters usually migrate into shallow waters during the spring and into deeper waters during the late fall. During the winter months, most of the population is off-shore in water depths as deep as 110 feet.

In April, as surface water temperatures warm up, the plastered females are the first to move inshore. The warmer water shortens the hatching time for their eggs. The males begin to show up in May, and before the end of the summer the migration is complete. In the fall, the animals will start moving back out into deeper water. This movement is usually initiated by storms or increased wave action.

Panulirus argus , a Caribbean cousin, is known to migrate great dis-tances in lines referred to as "marches." On the Pacific coast, small numbers of California spiny lobsters have been reported to march, too. Since *P. interruptus* is residential in nature, meaning they live in the same area for extended periods, shorter marches offshore and onshore

Habitat like this is where lobsters tend to move during the warmer fall months. The loss of habitat is damaging to the lobster population.

may occur. However, there are no scientific accounts of this behavior.

Reliable diver reports have been received of "bull rings." They are described as large male lobsters circled up on the sand with their tails towards the center and their antennae actively pointed outward. These reports support the theory of marches, since lobsters wouldn't normally be aggregated out in the open.

History of the Lobster Fishery

Richard Henry Dana who wrote the book, *Two Years Before the Mast*, about his travels by ship along the west coast, first wrote about recreational lobster fishing in San Diego Bay during the period 1834-1836. This was the first recorded account of lobsters being taken for sport.

In 1887, David Starr Jordan (a famous marine scientist) reported that "nearly all of the crawfish sold in San Francisco came from Santa Barbara. About 90 tons are taken annually." In the same period, average sized commercially caught lobsters weighed 3-1/2 to 4 pounds. Most lobsters sold today weigh half that much.

At the beginning of the twentieth century, the California Fish and Game Commission enacted a closed season, size limit, and a prohibition against taking females with eggs. Size limits continued to be adjusted, and a closed season between March 15th and early October has been in effect since 1935, to protect spiny lobsters when they're reproducing and molting.

Commercial fishermen use traps to capture spiny lobsters. Most traps are rectangular boxes of heavy wire mesh coated with tar. The traps are baited with fish carcasses or canned cat food, and are weighted with bricks or cement so that they rest on the ocean bottom. Each trap is marked with a buoy with a "P" followed by the fisherman's license number. Every trap is required to have a rectangular escape port (2-3/8 x 11-1/2 inches) so that undersize or "short" lobster can escape.

All traps used in California waters are required to have a "destruct device" so the door will fall open after a short period of time and the trap will no longer fish if it is lost. When traps are lost and continue to fish it is called "ghost fishing." Trappers will sometimes put out hundreds of traps depending on the size of their vessel and the amount of time they want to spend fishing.

It is illegal to disturb a commercial lobster trap, and it is also potentially dangerous. Divers have become entangled in traps and almost drowned. Stay away from commercial traps, and report traps that are fishing out of season or in protected areas to your nearest Fish

and Game office. The phone numbers for each office are listed in the current fishing regulation booklet.

Many traps are lost each season, primarily because of storms. Storm swells wash the traps in shallow water ashore and pound them into junk. In deeper water, they frequently are sanded in. Buoy lines and buoys are cut or lost, and then the trap can never be recovered.

Trappers must abide by the same size limit as recreational divers, 3-1/4 inches measured in a straight line on the mid-line of the back from the rear edge of the eye socket to the rear edge of the body shell. However, they have no limitation on the number of lobsters they can take. All lobsters are sold live to dealers who generally export them to Taiwan, Japan, China and France. More recently, there has been an effort to establish local live markets in southern California. However, most restaurants that serve spiny lobster are preparing frozen tails from the Caribbean and other tropical areas.

The commercial lobster fishery became limited entry in 1995. That means new participants are not allowed into the fishery until the number of permittees drops to the level most desirable for a sustainable fishery.

During the first few weeks of lobster season commercial landings are high. Landings then drop off and decline for the rest of the season. This is the same pattern seen in the recreational fishery. Commercial landings of California spiny lobster reached a peak of 1.1 million pounds in the 1949-50 season. This was followed by declining landings until the low of 155 thousand pounds was landed in 1974-75. Since then landings have increased and stabilized between 400 and

Biology of the California Spiny Lobster

600 thousand pounds. The price paid to the fisherman at the dock (ex-vessel) has been increasing and is now in the $7.00-$8.00 range. The retail price may be as much as double the ex-vessel price. The three major port areas are San Diego, Los Angeles/Orange and Santa Barbara/Ventura counties.

The recreational catch is impossible to determine under current regulations. Fishermen use hoop nets from small boats and the shore, and skin and scuba divers access the ocean from shore, private boats, and commercial passenger dive vessels.

Log books are required from the commercial passenger dive boat fleet. However, what portion of the recreational catch they take is unknown.

Commercial lobster trappers are required to log their catch, both legal and "shorts" (undersize lobster), every day they pull their traps.

Chapter 3
Lobster Diving Regulations

The California Department of Fish and Game regulates the recreational lobster diving fishery throughout the state, and it is your responsibility to check the latest regulations. While the regulations have not changed in the years immediately prior to the publication of this book, the laws CAN and DO change. It is up to you to make sure you know the latest regulations.

Certain aspects of the law have not changed in many years, such as the legal size a lobster must be and the legal methods of capture. In this section we will point out the parts of the law that have remained fairly constant and those that are more subject to change.

California Sport Fishing Regulations

Each year, the Department of Fish and Game publishes a booklet with the details of the sport fishing regulations. The booklet is free and can be obtained from most tackle shops, sport fish landings, dive shops, and from most Department offices. In addition, most dive boats carry at least one copy of the regulations on board.

Keep in mind that the regulation booklets are not always published on January 1, because the regulations change at odd times of the year. For example, in the year 2000, the booklet with the regulations became effective on March 1 and is supposed to be valid until February 28, 2002. However, under the effective date

Be sure to get a copy of the California Sport Fishing Regulations each year. This is a free publication.

the book also includes the following note, "unless otherwise noted herein."

The Department also publishes supplements to the regulations, at irregular intervals, of laws that have changed. Be sure to check for supplements at the start of each lobster season.

Your Fishing License

Although you are not required to carry a fishing license with you underwater, you are required to have your license with you in an immediately accessible location any time you are diving for lobsters. You can keep your license aboard the boat, or in your car if you are beach diving. However, it's not sufficient to tell the warden that your license is at home. You must have it with you at the location where your dive originated (such as on the boat or in your car).

Even if a warden knows you and has seen your license on previous occasions, you may still receive a ticket if you do not have your license with you and have lobsters in your possession. Don't take a chance; always have a current license and carry it with you whenever you go diving. The license year is from January 1 to December 31, so remember that the license you started the season with in October will need to be replaced if you dive any time after the first of the year and before the end of lobster season.

You must exhibit your fishing license to any game warden or other peace officer who asks you to produce it.

You May Only Take Lobsters By Hand

In California, you may only take lobsters by using your hands. As a diver, you may NOT net, spear, gig, hook, trap, or use any implement other than your hands to capture lobsters in California.

In the year 2000 the law specifically reads, "...skin and SCUBA divers may take crustaceans by the use of the hands except divers may not possess any hooked device while diving or attempting to dive."

Although divers in Florida use gigs, it is strictly illegal to do so in California. This law has not changed since divers first began diving for lobsters in California, and it is highly unlikely it will change in the future.

Lobster Season Runs from Early October through mid-March

The current lobster season for recreational divers runs from the Saturday preceding the first Wednesday in October through the first

Wardens, like Mike Ferrence, have heard just about every excuse under the sun. The bottom line: don't get a ticket for a Fish and Game violation!

Wednesday after the 15th of March. This season is only slightly different from the old season that was in effect for many years.

Sport divers got a bonus of four extra days of diving over the commercial lobster fishermen in the mid-90s. While it seems likely that the season as currently defined will continue for the foreseeable future, there is always the possibility this could change. Be sure to check the regulations annually for changes in the season.

The Legal Limit is Seven Lobsters Per Day

Unless you have an extremely large family, seven lobsters is more than enough to feed most households. Considering how rich lobsters are to eat, one lobster will usually feed two people when accompanied by vegetables and a salad. While the original limit for sport diving was 10 lobsters per day, the number was decreased to seven in 1971.

This limit could be changed at any time if the Department of Fish and Game or the public felt the lobster population was in decline. Be sure to check the limit annually.

If you go on a multi-day boat trip you can obtain a multi-day permit that will allow you to take a limit for each day that you are away from shore, for up to three days. If you are on a charter boat, be sure to check with the skipper to see if they have such a permit. You can get a multi-day permit for a private boat as well, but you must apply for the permit and receive it, before you leave for your trip. There is a fee for a multi-day permit. Contact your local Department of Fish and Game office to apply for this type of permit.

Keep in mind that even with a multi-day permit, you are still limited to seven lobsters per day. You can't catch 21 lobsters on the first day of a three day trip. If you do, and a warden boards the boat on the second day, you will get a ticket.

Know the Minimum Size

The minimum size for a California spiny lobster in the year 2000 is "three and one fourth inches measured in a straight line on the midline of the back from the rear edge of the eye socket to the rear edge of the body shell." You must use an accurate metal or plastic gauge to check this measurement. See the drawing on page 28 for the correct area of measurement.

This size limit has been in effect for many years and seems unlikely to change. Still, it is wise to check the regulations each year to be sure that no change has occurred.

The law requires that you measure your lobster before you place it in a bag or bring it aboard your boat. You may bring a lobster to the surface to measure it, but this is a waste of your time and your air. Measure your lobster underwater; make sure it's legal size, and put it in your bag.

The original provision for bringing a lobster to the surface to measure it was written at a time when most diving for lobsters was done by skin divers who did not use scuba. It was thought reasonable, at that time, to allow a breath-hold diver to catch a lobster and bring it to the surface to measure it without a penalty if it was undersize.

Bringing your lobster to the surface to measure it is a bad move for the lobster if you discover it is "short." If you release the lobster at the surface it will likely fall prey to any number of creatures that want to eat it on its trip back to the bottom. The end result is that there will be one less lobster to breed and less lobsters to catch in the future. Always measure your lobster on the bottom. It's the sportsmanlike thing to do.

Upsizing is Illegal

It's not uncommon for a good lobster diver to get a limit of lobsters early in the day, only to see larger lobsters later in the day. In this situation, there's a natural tendency to want to "trade" in your smaller

Warden Santos Cabral shows the correct technique for measuring a lobster. This one is definitely "short!" (© John Suchil. All rights reserved.)

lobsters for larger ones. This is illegal because at some point during this exercise you will have more than seven lobsters in your possession and will have exceeded the limit. This practice is known as "upsizing" and is frowned upon by game wardens and environmentally conscious hunters.

You Can't Sell Your Catch

It is illegal for you to sell sport caught lobsters. This is a serious violation of the Fish and Game Code, known as "market hunting," and you will receive a ticket and fine for this offense.

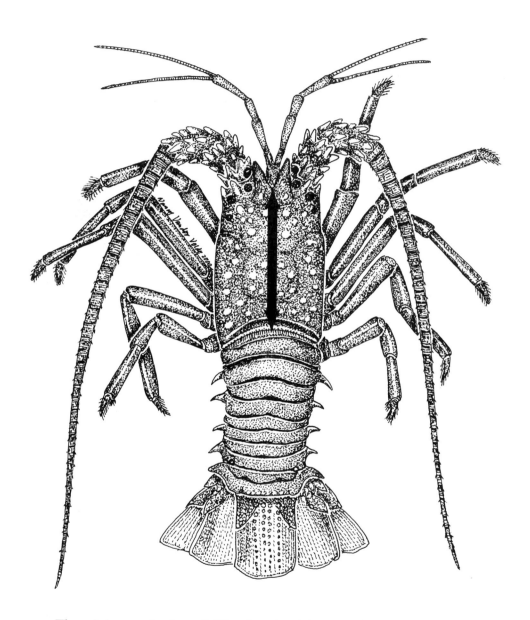

The minimum size for a California spiny lobster in the year 2000 is "three and one-fourth inches measured in a straight line on the mid-line of the back from the rear edge of the eye socket to the rear edge of the body shell." You must use an accurate metal or plastic gauge to check this measurement.

The size of the lobster in this dimension **must** **exceed** the size of the gauge. If the gauge fits between the eye sockets and slips over the end of the carapace, the lobster is undersized.

Chapter 4
Lobster Diving Gear

Successful lobster diving requires skill more than anything else, but it doesn't hurt to have the right accessories. While a good lobster hunter can get by with almost any set of gloves or game bag, certain types of gear will make your hunt undeniably easier. In this chapter, we'll look at some of the gear that will make your lobster grabbing more successful and enjoyable.

The fundamental accessories you'll need for California lobster diving includes a pair of gloves, a goody bag, a measuring device, and a fishing license. Additional items that can make the difference in a productive day of diving include a dive light, weight belt clips, stainless steel or brass rings, and retractors. For night diving, you'll also want a diver marking light.

Gloves Protect Your Hands

The selection of dive gloves available today is truly staggering, but not all gloves are good for lobster diving. While selecting gloves is a matter of personal choice, the wrong type of gloves can slow you down and make handling lobsters difficult.

While the main purpose of your gloves will be to protect your hands, the palms of the gloves should provide a firm grip on the lobster. Yet, for lobster diving you need gloves that will also allow you to change your grip easily. Gloves made from foam neoprene (wetsuit material) with a foam neoprene palm are not well suited to lobster diving.

The problem with foam neoprene gloves (with foam neoprene palms) is that the spines on the lobster's carapace will get stuck in the glove, making it difficult or impossible to reposition your hand on the lobster's body. This can cause frustration when you have an insecure grip on a lobster and want to work your hand into a better position before you pull the animal out of its hole.

In warmer waters, you can use almost any type of glove that has a slick palm, such as a plastic glove or leather glove. These gloves are inexpensive and readily available at most hardware stores. Leather is not the best choice, however, because leather gloves have a tendency

Lobster Diving Gear

Gloves are essential for lobster diving.

to become loose in the water and harden when they dry.

Gloves that have a neoprene back and a synthetic leather palm are probably the best all-around gloves for lobster diving. The neoprene will help to keep your hands warm while the synthetic material will help to protect your hands while allowing you to change your grip more easily. Another type of glove that is popular has a neoprene back with a Kevlar® palm and fingers.

Gloves should fit snugly without being excessively tight. The gloves should extend far enough up your wrist to cover and protect your skin when you reach into holes.

Even the best gloves will not completely protect your hands from punctures from lobster spines, rocks, and sea urchins. In the excitement of the hunt, you'll probably end up with some minor nicks and cuts as you wrestle your lobsters out of their holes. Most divers don't seem to mind this too much, especially after they've bagged a truly big bug!

Goody Bags

Goody bags are deceptively simple pieces of gear, but there are several on the market that can make the difference between bagging and keeping your bugs and losing them. Almost every lobster diver we know has lost a lobster at one time or other because of a poorly designed goody bag.

When you select a goody bag there are several things you should keep in mind. The best goody bags have the following features:
- They can be opened easily with one hand.
- They can be closed easily with one hand.
- Lobsters can be loaded into the bag without allowing lobsters

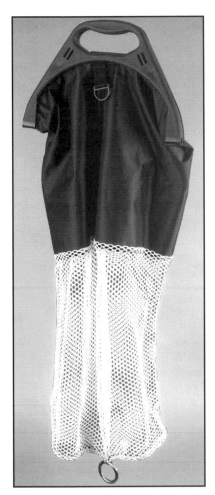

The upper part of this bag is plastic while the lower part is mesh.

Any goody bag you use for lobster diving should be capable of being opened with one hand. Note the spring loaded handle on this bag that makes it convenient to use.

already in the bag to escape.
   • The bag has the minimum amount of drag.

   Even though you dive with a buddy, you'll want a goody bag that can be operated with one hand. If you get into a hot spot, your buddy may be busy trying to bag his own lobster. There are several different types of bags that feature single-handed operation.
   The two most efficient lobster bags on the market have different designs. One is spring-loaded and the other has a slit in the side that only allows lobsters to slide in one direction.

Lobster Diving Gear

This bag has a slit or "tunnel" that will only allow you to insert the lobsters into the bag tail first. A zipper along the bottom edge of the bag makes it easy to remove lobsters after the dive.

Bags made completely of mesh are ideal for storing your lobsters between dives.

The spring-loaded bag has a handle (see photo on prior page) that can be squeezed to open the mouth of the bag. When you load a lobster into this type of bag, you must shake the bag to be sure that any previously captured lobsters are in the bottom of the bag or else they may escape. When you release the handle, the mouth of the bag snaps shut. It's quick and easy to use.

The bag with a slit takes a slightly different approach. The slit is in the side of the bag and the material overlaps forming a snug "tunnel" through which you insert your lobsters into the bag. Lobsters must be inserted tail first into the bag; otherwise their spines will catch on the material and make it difficult to stuff them in. This type of sack is equipped with a zipper along the bottom to make it easy to remove your lobsters from the bag once you're back on deck. Just be sure to zip it closed before you enter the water on your next dive or you'll end up losing your catch.

Less sophisticated and less expensive mesh and canvas bags can also be used underwater, but they are slower to use and you stand a bigger chance of losing a lobster when you use these types of bags. Canvas bags have more drag than mesh or nylon bags.

Most serious lobster divers have more than one goody bag. The main reason for this is that if you are diving off a boat and plan to make multiple dives, you'll want somewhere to store the lobsters from your first dive. It's silly to carry all your lobsters from earlier dives with you, unless it makes you feel good to have them keep you company!

Lobsters collected during previous dives can be kept alive by placing them in a second bag that can be hung over the side of the boat if you're diving from a small boat. Large charter dive boats, frequently have a game tank (live well) where you can store your goody bag until the boat returns to port. Just be sure your bag is marked in some way so you can identify it as yours.

Your second bag can be any type of inexpensive goody bag, although we tend to prefer a canvas bag or plastic bag with a mesh bottom. There are two main reasons to use a canvas bag to store your lobsters between dives, durability and travel. First, spiny lobsters seem to tear up mesh bags rather quickly and canvas or plastic bags seem to last longer in this application. Canvas bags stay damp longer than mesh bags, which can help keep your lobsters alive during the trip home in the car. Additionally, it's easy to mark a canvas or plastic bag by writing your name on the side of it with a waterproof marker.

If you hang your bag over the side of the boat to keep your lobster's alive, be sure to pull the bag back in before the boat moves to the next dive site or heads home. More than one diver has forgotten their bag and had their lobsters chopped to bits by the propeller of a boat!

Measuring Devices are the Law

The law requires that every diver who takes lobsters must have an approved measuring device, or "gauge," for measuring their catch underwater. It is not legal to bring your lobster aboard the boat to measure it, nor is it legal to place a lobster into a "receiver" (i.e., goody bag) without measuring it to determine whether it is legal size. Many wardens for the Department of Fish and Game are divers, and it is not unusual for them to watch unsuspecting divers underwater and ticket them for failing to follow the law.

Lobster measuring devices should be of thin, stamped metal that allows the device to easily slide between the horns of the lobster. In the past, some manufacturers produced plastic gauges designed to meas-

Lobster Diving Gear

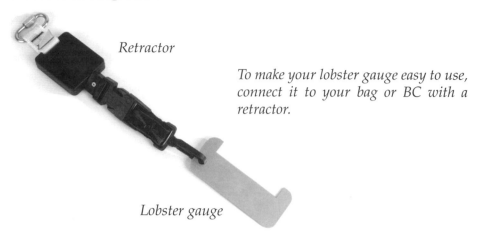

Retractor

To make your lobster gauge easy to use, connect it to your bag or BC with a retractor.

Lobster gauge

ure both lobsters and abalone. These gauges were sometimes made from thick material that would hang up between the horns of the lobster. Lobsters measured with these gauges could actually be too short. If you own one of these gauges, you should not use it for measuring lobsters.

Don't be tempted to save a small amount of money and try to make your own gauge unless you are good with tools and have access to very accurate measuring equipment. Wardens carry especially accurate gauges, and if your gauge is undersize because you made it yourself, you will receive a ticket.

It's a good idea to carry at least one extra measuring gauge with you at all times. We've had gauges break and we've lost gauges. For this reason, we usually have an extra gauge clipped to our goody bag, as well as another spare attached to our storage bag aboard the boat. If you are stopped by a game warden and you have no gauge, the fact that you lost your gauge is not considered an acceptable excuse for not having one.

Fishing Licenses are Mandatory

Almost everyone needs to have a fishing license to take lobsters. The only exceptions are children under the age of 16. Everyone else must have a license, including visitors from out of state. If you are a visitor you must still buy a license.

A new license must be purchased every year. Since lobster season runs from early October to mid-March most years, it's not uncommon for divers to forget to purchase a new license when they dive just after the first of the year. Don't get caught without a license! The fines for taking game without a license are quite steep and can run into the hundreds of dollars, depending on where you are and how much game you have in your possession at the time you are cited.

Dive Lights Will Help You Get Lobsters During the Day, Too!

Most divers don't realize it, but a dive light will help you find lobsters during the daytime, too. This is especially true on overcast days, but a good light is a valuable resource almost any time. Anyone who is serious about lobster diving will carry a light during daytime hours, too.

Although most lobsters can usually be found at the entrance to their holes during daylight hours, a light can prove invaluable for deep holes, holes with more than one lobster in them, and for checking out the "back door" of a hole. In addition, a light beam swung over the face of a reef will highlight any lobsters that are there and draw your attention to them. In some cases, you can also use a light to distract a lobster while you use your free hand to grab it.

Keep in mind that just because you have a light doesn't mean that you should feel that it's safe to enter caves or caverns in search of lobsters if you have not been trained in cave or cavern diving techniques. Many of the caves and caverns at the offshore islands are full of silt and are as complex as any cave found in Florida or Mexico. Many divers have been killed because they have become lost in caves off the coast of California. Don't enter a cave unless you are trained to do so and have all of the proper equipment.

Today's dive lights are exceptionally rugged, offer tremendous reliability, and provide long bulb and battery life. If you limit your diving to daytime hunts, you can get by with a small light that operates

Serious bug divers always carry a light with them, even during the day.

Lobster Diving Gear

Just because you carry a light doesn't mean you are qualified to enter a cave in search of lobsters. Many divers have lost their lives in underwater caves in search of lobsters. Don't make the same mistake!

on four c-cells or less. If you are a serious night diver, you'll want a light with greater capability as your primary light as well as at least one smaller light to serve as your back-up light.

Features to Look for in a Dive Light

Everyone has their own preferences, but when you select a light for lobster diving, the following features seem to work best:

- Sinking Light
- Dual bulbs
- Lanyard
- Head-mounted lights
- Narrow beam
- Lens protector
- Smallest light that will do the job

Although some divers prefer a floating light, thinking they won't ever lose a light that floats, we think this is faulty logic. There are many times when you will want to set your light aside, because you need both hands to drag a big bug out of a hole. If you have a floating light, it will simply float away and you may never find it if currents or wind cause it to drift off. If your light sinks, you can just set it down

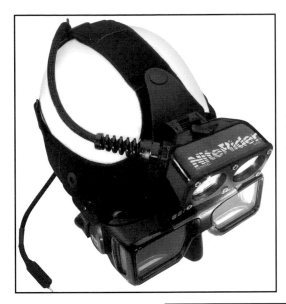

A head mounted light is the ultimate "hands-free" dive light. (© NiteRider. All rights reserved.)

Small lights like these tuck easily into a BC pocket.

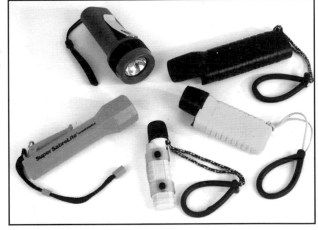

on the bottom next to you until you are done wrestling your lobster.

Some lights that float have the option to allow you to weight them so they will sink. If your light has this capability, be sure to weight it so you don't lose it.

While you might think a wide beam is the ideal light source, we've generally found that a more narrow, focused beam provides sufficient light in most cases to get the job done. This allows you to use a much smaller light in most cases. It's easy and quick to pan your light back and forth as you swim along the bottom.

For night diving, new divers usually feel more secure with a big light, but with today's highly efficient dive lights, this is usually unnecessary. For lobster diving, the smaller the light you can use, the better. A big light will usually accomplish nothing more than to get in your way once you have your hands on a lobster.

One very good feature that's available on some lights today is a dual bulb system that allows you to switch to a second bulb underwater if the first one burns out. This is an excellent idea and certainly worth considering if you're in the market for a light.

A rubber lens protector is another desirable feature that will help to protect your light when you're working among the rocks. This will help extend the life of your light.

Don't even think of taking a hand-held dive light underwater without a lanyard or some way to attach the light to your buoyancy compensator. Whatever method you use, it must allow you to instantly detach the light in the event it becomes entangled with anything underwater.

Divers who do lots of night diving should consider a head-mounted light. These can be as simple as a small flashlight clipped to your mask strap or as sophisticated as a heavy-duty battery pack with a cable providing power to a small head-mounted bulb and reflector. Head-mounted lights are the ultimate "hands-free" option for lobster diving.

Rigging Your Bag and Weight Belt

Carrying a lobster bag in your hand at your side is inefficient and creates a lot of drag. This will slow your progress through the water and lead to fatigue. On the surface, it is almost impossible to swim through thick kelp if you have a bag full of lobsters in your hand. By rigging your weight belt and bag to work as a system, you become much more efficient.

The first step in setting up your gear is to purchase a two inch diameter brass or stainless steel ring, two plastic cable ties, two brass snap hooks designed for sliding on to a weight belt, and four weight stoppers. If your dive store doesn't carry the rings try the local marine hardware supply store.

Fasten the ring to the bottom of your goody bag using the cable ties by threading the ties through the mesh on the bottom of the bag and around the ring. Tighten the ties and cut off any excess "tail" from the ties. File the sharp end of the "tail" until it is smooth.

To rig your belt, attach a brass snap hook on the left and right side of your weight belt, using the weight stoppers to prevent them from sliding around. You may have to experiment a bit to get the position exactly right. To check the position, fill the bag with some towels to simulate a bag full of lobsters. Don your weight belt, clip the handle

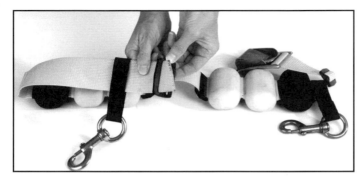

Rig the weight stoppers.

This belt is properly rigged with weight stoppers and brass clips.

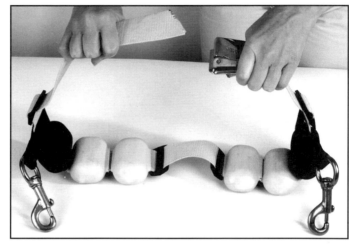

of the bag to one of the snap hooks, pass the bag behind your butt, and attach the other snap hook to the ring on the bottom of the bag. The ring on the bag should easily reach the second snap hook. If it doesn't, you'll need to reposition the snap hooks so they are the proper distance apart.

Some divers prefer to mount the brass rings on their belt and the snap clip on the bag. They feel this makes one-handed operation easier. You may need to experiment to see which technique works best for you, but either method is better than carrying your bag by hand.

When you are swimming through the water, the bag may be clipped to your belt in this manner, whether it is empty or full. This makes it easy to swim, particularly if you must swim on the surface over thick kelp. With some bags, (when the bag is empty) you can also wrap the tail end of the bag back into the open end and clip the bag shut to create less drag for swimming

When you are underwater and you have located lobsters, it's easy to unclip the bag for loading. Once you've loaded your catch into the bag, clip the handle and bottom of the bag to the snap hooks and you're on your way.

Lobster Diving Gear

Clip the top of the goody bag to one of the brass snap hooks on your weight belt and pass the bag behind you. Note that Kristine is wearing a weight harness and this method still works.

Clip the ring on the bottom of the bag to the snap hook on the opposite side of your weight belt. If you're using a weight integrated BC you can rig a separate belt just for this purpose with no weights, just the clips.

Brass clip connected to ring on bag

Kristine has her goody bag rigged with brass clips so that she doesn't have to carry it in her hand.

Retractors Help Make Diving Easy

Retractors are spring-loaded devices with waterproof cables that mount on your buoyancy compensator and connect to your accessories, such as a small light or your lobster gauge. When you want to use the accessory, you pull it away from the retractor and the cable unreels. When you are finished using the accessory, you simply release it and the retractor reels it back in.

Better retractors use stainless steel cables rather than nylon cables. Nylon cables can break causing you to lose your gear.

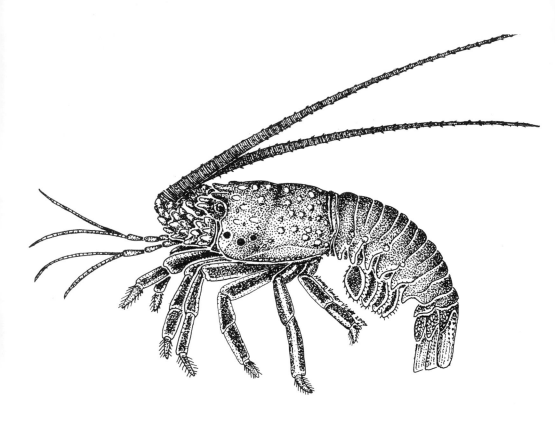

Chapter 5
Lobster Diving Techniques

Some people catch more lobsters than others due to skill, instinct, and luck. It's not uncommon for a new diver to not even see lobsters on the same dive where an experienced diver might come back with a limit. If you're a novice diver, just because you don't see any lobsters doesn't mean they aren't in the area. We've been in areas where few people came back with any lobsters, yet the experienced divers returned with big bugs. Don't get discouraged, just keep looking!

To be a successful lobster diver requires a combination of recognizing likely habitat, aggressiveness, and luck. Almost anyone can learn to be a good lobster diver with practice.

Learn to think like a lobster and imagine where you would be if you were a lobster. How would you hide if you were a lobster? How would you escape if a big, bubble-blowing predator were chasing you?

Successful lobster diving requires three different sets of skills: locating the lobsters, catching them, and bagging the lobsters. You must learn to be good in all three areas if you want to bring lobsters home for dinner.

Locating Lobsters

Locating lobsters is in some ways the most critical of all lobster diving skills. If you can't find the lobsters in the first place, you won't have the opportunity to catch them.

Unless you happen to find a "glory hole," a spot that's crawling with lobsters, the first rule of lobster diving is to cover as much ground as possible. If you're not seeing lobsters, you must keep moving. The more bottom you cover, the more chance there is that you will find an area where lobsters are living.

To start your lobster hunt, look for rocky habitat with lots of holes and jumbled rock. Lobsters prefer rocky habitat with plenty of places to hide since their only defense is their spiny body. Don't waste time searching on a sandy bottom or in area with no holes for the lobsters to retreat into.

Once you see your first lobster, slow down and look around carefully. There probably are others close by.

In some areas, particularly along the coast, there seems to be a relationship between lobsters and garibaldi. Skip Dunham, one of the most successful lobster divers we know, refers to garibaldi as "lobster flags," meaning if you see a garibaldi, there's likely to be a lobster close by. While this won't always be true, it's another indicator you should program into your brain to help you when you're hunting.

Once you see a lobster, slow down and look around. Generally speaking, if one lobster has found an area to be good habitat, it's quite likely that other lobsters will be in the immediate vicinity. Take care not to disturb the other lobsters around you as you wrestle your first one into the bag.

As you prepare to grab your first lobster, look around and see where the other lobsters are near you. If you're really good, you will be planning your next grab even as you bag your first bug.

Since lobsters move around during the season, you need to keep in mind that an area that is a good spot one week may have no lobsters the next. In the fall, when the weather is mild and there is no big surf or rain, look for lobsters in water as shallow as six feet in the surf grass beds.

As the weather changes, lobsters "walk," or move out into deeper water. In November they may be in water depths down to 40 or 50 feet. In the mid-winter, after big storms or heavy rain, look for lobsters as deep as 110 feet. Keep in mind that the habits of animals change greatly in response to weather variations, and during an El Niño or La Niña event they may behave in ways that are unexpected. For example, the migration of lobsters from shallow to deep water may be early or late due to variations in the weather.

If the habitat looks good but you're not seeing lobsters try moving either deeper or shallower. If they are not deep, move shallow. If they are not shallow, move deep. Of course, you must monitor your no-decompression status carefully if you move from shallow to deep water.

As you swim along the reef, sweep your dive light over the entrances to holes and crevices. Even during the daytime, your light will make the red of the lobster's body stand out from the rest of the reef.

Sometimes you will see the entire lobster sitting out in front of its hole. Usually, you will see only the antennae, or even just the tips of the antennae. In most instances, if you have to look deep into a hole to see a lobster you're probably not going to be able to get to it anyway. Don't your waste time probing every hole along the reef. If there are

Sweep your light over the rocks and keep moving if you're not seeing any lobsters.

Don't waste a lot of time looking into deep holes. If the lobsters aren't where you can grab them, keep moving.

lobsters there you should be able to see them.

Novice divers frequently are so overwhelmed with visual stimuli from the dive they will fail to see lobsters right in front of them. As you become more relaxed and at home in the water you will begin to be able to pick out lobsters from all of the other visual "noise" surrounding them.

If you dive an area and see only "short" (undersize) lobsters, be sure to write the information in your logbook and visit the same area next year. If it is good habitat, the lobsters will return and some of the ones that were too small this year may be legal size next year.

Catching Lobsters

Everyone has a different technique for grabbing lobsters, and you will undoubtedly develop your own style. The key is to try different techniques and see what works for you. Once you begin to have success, evaluate what you did and work on improving that technique.

When you see a lobster, slow down and take a good look at it. Before you grab a lobster, take a moment to evaluate the situation, but don't spend all day sizing it up. If you wait too long and make a ruckus you may make the lobster "nervous" and spook it. Sometimes it's best to launch an immediate attack because they will often move towards you when they first see you.

Most bug divers prefer to be a bit negatively buoyant when they are wrestling a lobster. This will provide you with more control, particularly if there is surge or you are breathing heavily. If you have the time, vent a bit of air from your BC just before you go into "attack mode."

In evaluating a lobster the first thing to consider is its size. Take a good look and make sure it's a legal lobster before you grab it. As a beginner, you'll probably have a hard time judging whether a lobster is legal or not just by looking at it. Most beginners end up grabbing a few short lobsters and releasing them before they can "eyeball" a lobster and tell whether it is legal or not. Even experienced divers usually make mistakes at the beginning of the season and end up grabbing a few shorts before their eyeballs kick into the proper gear.

Grabbing short lobsters is bad for several reasons. From a purely biological perspective, grabbing a short lobster is usually bad for the lobster. In most cases, novice divers who grab lobsters almost always end up injuring the lobster, either by breaking off its antenna or breaking legs. When this happens, the lobster becomes more vulnerable to attack by other marine creatures. In addition, an injured lobster grows more slowly and any energy that it might use for growth is redirected towards repairing its injured body part.

From a diving standpoint, wrestling a short lobster is unproductive and a total waste of your air and bottom time. Most divers use a lot of air when they become excited and grab a lobster. If you're grabbing shorts and spending any time doing it, you've wasted time you could devote to locating and grabbing legal lobsters.

When you grab a lobster you must be quick and aggressive. A slow, timid grab will not get you a lobster. You have to be fast and you have to take the offensive. You can't worry too much about sea urchin spines or rocks in your way. Anyone who is serious about grabbing lobsters will inevitably end up with nicks, cuts, and sea urchin spines in their hands. If you make a half-hearted grab, the lobster will be gone. Your grab needs to be a lightening-like strike.

Once you have located a lobster and determined that it is legal, take a moment to plan your grab. Every grab will be different based upon the size of the lobster and the structure of the hole. The best situation you can hope for during a daytime dive is a big lobster in a shallow hole with a wide opening and no "back door" for the lobster to escape. If there is nowhere for the lobster to go, you simply grab the lobster and drag him out of the hole. It's easy, but is usually the least common situation you will encounter.

The worst case situation is a lobster in a deep hole with a tight

If a lobster wedges himself into a hole, sometimes you can reach in and shake him loose.

opening. If you miss the lobster on the first grab, he will shoot back into the hole and will probably be beyond your grasp. Unless you can reach the lobster easily, don't waste your time waiting for him to come back out.

Sometimes you can fool a lobster by using one hand as a decoy to distract the lobster's attention while using your other hand to make the grab. The shining bulb of a dive light is a good distraction.

If you're going to use a one hand grab, your grab should be aimed for the back of the lobster's carapace, close to the tail, or even slightly behind the lobster, depending on how quick you can move. The lobster will generally start to move as soon as he senses your movement. Even if you aim for the back of the carapace, your hand will usually end up somewhere closer to the animal's head. Use a one-hand grab when the opening of the hole is tight, or your other hand is occupied holding a light or holding yourself stable against a rock in the surge.

When the opening to the hole is large, you may want to use two hands, if you're comfortable with this technique. Bring your hands in rapidly from both sides, again aiming to grab the carapace.

Never try to grab a lobster if all you can reach are the antennae. The antennae are extremely delicate and will break off as the lobster jerks backwards. Without antennae, the lobster is unable to sense predators effectively and will end up becoming lunch for another marine creature.

When you grab a lobster, you need to pin it to the bottom first rather than immediately pulling it out of the hole. Once you have it pinned, make sure your grip is secure before trying to remove it from its home. If you can get a second hand on it, be sure to do so, especially if it is a large bug.

Quite often, you'll grab a lobster as he moves back into the hole and establish a grip on the body that prevents it from escaping but does not allow you to pull the lobster out of the hole. When a lobster is trapped in a small crevice, it will usually extend its legs and arch its tail in an effort to prevent you from dragging it out of the hole.

To subdue the lobster, the first thing you will need to do is reposition your hand while maintaining a tight grip. This can be tricky, as you need to move your hand over the spiny surface of the carapace while not losing your grip. If the lobster senses your grip loosening at all, he will usually thrash his tail in an effort to escape.

It's also not uncommon to grab a lobster with an incomplete grip holding the base of a single antenna. In this situation, you need to get a grip on the base of both antennae before you try to remove the lobster from its hole. Just be sure you have a good grip on the base of the antennae where they connect to the body. This will provide you with excellent control of the animal.

You must keep a firm grip on your bug at all times!

Lobster Diving Techniques

Once you have a good grip on the base of the antennae, usually referred to as the "knuckles," you can start to shake and twist the lobster vigorously. Shaking the lobster accomplishes two things; first, you will physically break the lobster's "grip" in the rocks, and secondly, if you shake the lobster hard enough, you will disorient him and make it easier to remove him from the hole.

As you shake the lobster, and feel his grip loosening on the sides of the rocks, start pulling him towards you. Be sure to keep your grip as tight as possible because the moment he clears the hole, he will usually start to flap his tail in an effort to escape. If you loosen your grip even momentarily the lobster will probably vanish.

If you miss a lobster, sometimes if you stir up the silt in the bottom of the hole, they will come out looking for a better place to hide. This doesn't occur too often, and you shouldn't waste a great deal of time waiting for this to happen. If the lobster doesn't come out of the hole within 30-45 seconds, move on and look for another one. You can always come back by that way and check the situation out again towards the end of your dive.

In a situation where the lobster is in a hole with a back exit (door), there are several ways to deal with this. If your buddy is not busy with his own lobster, have him cover the back door for you. In many cases, the lobster will scoot right into his hand if you miss your grab. Or, if your buddy is preoccupied, you can plug the back door with a rock so the lobster can't escape. If the hole is small and the distance between the front door and the back isn't great, you can use one hand to chase the lobster to your other hand. Grabbing a lobster from behind is always easier than grabbing a lobster from the front.

If you accidentally lose your grip on your lobster, and he takes off and you didn't see where he went, check your chest first. Sometimes, if you are wearing a black wetsuit, the bug will come right back to you, thinking that your black wetsuit is the opening to a dark hole. This doesn't always happen, but its worth a quick feel to see if that's what happened.

If you see the bug scooting away from you, follow it if you can. In most cases, the bug won't be able to immediately find a hole to duck into and you'll get a chance at another grab. This second chance is often better that the first, because usually the bug is out in the open, or down in a pile of rocks with nowhere to go. In this situation, grab the lobster from behind, measure him, and stuff him quickly into your bag.

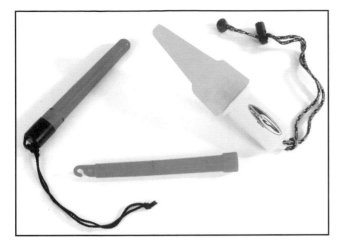

Chemical lightsticks and resusable lights are used to mark your position at night.

Night Diving

Catching lobsters at night is much easier than catching lobsters during the day. At night, they come out of their holes and crawl around on the bottom in search of food. This makes it much easier to grab them than when they are holed up. Of course, you must be trained in night diving techniques to dive efficiently after dark.

When you see a lobster crawling out in the open at night, keep your light shined in its eyes. This will effectively blind it, temporarily. Move in towards the lobster staying up off the bottom. If you land on the bottom and kick up lots of sand, the lobster will be alerted to your presence and quickly move away.

As you shine your light at the lobster's eyes, bring your free hand around and grab the lobster from behind on the carapace. If you are working as an effective buddy team, you can have your partner swoop in from the rear and grab the lobster.

Measuring Your Lobster

Once you have your lobster in hand, you'll want to bag it as quickly as possible after measuring it. Remember, you must measure the lobster underwater, before you put it in the bag. You can be ticketed if you have short lobsters in your bag, even if you are underwater.

A lobster of any size must be kept under control while you measure it. If you don't feel you can effectively control the lobster by grabbing the knuckles you may want to place the lobster on a rock. Use one hand to hold the carapace of the lobster while your other hand grabs the tail. You must press down on the tail so that the lobster can't kick and escape. Use your free hand to grab your gauge and measure the bug.

Always be sure to measure your lobster before you place it in the bag. It is illegal to have short lobsters in your possession, even underwater!

Measure a lobster by placing one end of the open side of the gauge in the notch between the two horns on the lobster. Drop the gauge straight back towards the tail of the lobster along the midline of the carapace. The open mouth of the gauge should not fit over the end of the carapace where the tail begins. If it does, the lobster is too short. The carapace must be longer than the open mouth of the gauge.

You must be forceful to get your lobster into the bag. They will grab onto anything they can, including your gear, to try to avoid going into the bag. It is not uncommon for the lobster to lose legs as you work it into the bag.

Lobster Diving Techniques

Bagging Your Lobster

With a traditional bag, open the bag and put the lobster into the bag tail first, as you close the opening of the bag tightly around your hand. Release your grip on the lobster and it will shoot into the bottom of the bag. Keep pressure on the bag opening as you slide your hand out of the bag. Fasten the clip on the handle right away to keep the bag closed.

If you catch a big lobster and you need both hands to control it, you'll need help from your buddy if you don't have a bag that can be operated with one hand. Even if it is not a particularly large lobster, you may want help from your buddy if you are using an ordinary lobster bag, to help prevent any lobsters already in the bag from escaping.

With a traditional bag that already has lobsters in it, you need to force all of the lobsters into the bottom of the bag before you open the bag to prevent any of your catch from escaping. If your buddy is not immediately available because he is wrestling with his own lobster, as is often the case, shake the bag so that the lobsters fall towards the bottom of the bag. When you are sure that all of the lobsters are in the lower half of the bag, put the bag between your legs and clamp your thighs around the middle of the bag. If you're sure that all the lobsters are in the bottom half of the bag, open the bag and put your most recent capture inside. Close the bag around your hand as you slide your hand out of the bag.

If you have a bag with the tunnel opening, all you have to do is slide the lobster into the bag through the tunnel tail first. Just be sure that the zipper on the bottom of the bag is closed! We have almost lost lobsters by leaving the zipper on the bottom open…

Between Dives

If you are diving from a boat and plan to make multiple dives, you'll want to keep your lobsters alive while you continue to hunt. Transfer your catch from your first dive to your storage goody bag and hang it over the side or place it in the "live-well" of the boat. The "live-well" is a storage tank with fresh circulating seawater designed for holding live game. Most charter boats have live-wells; just ask the captain or deckhand where they are located on the boat.

If your bag is hanging over the side, remember to pull your bag back in whenever the boat is moved or when you depart for home at the end of the day.

Transporting Your Lobster

Lobsters are hardy creatures and can survive for many hours out of the water, provided they are kept cold. For transporting lobsters any distance, a canvas bag seems to work best because it will keep the lobsters damp and cool as the water evaporates.

Never leave your lobsters lying in the sun during a long boat trip on a hot day. Once a lobster dies bacteria will quickly start to grow. For safety, lobsters should be cooked or frozen while they are still live whenever possible.

Be sure to keep your lobsters alive by keeping them wet between dives. If you hang your bag over the back of the boat, be sure to pull it in when the boat leaves the dive site.

It takes just as much skill (perhaps more?) to capture a small lobster as a large one. Dive instructor Ed Stetson holds the monster in the front, while store owner and instructor Curt Wiessner holds the smaller bug in the rear.
(© John C. Black. All rights reserved.)

Chapter 6
Cooking, Cleaning,
and Eating Lobsters

Of all the seafood you can prepare, lobsters are one of the easiest and quickest. It is much simpler to cook and clean a lobster than it is to fillet and cook most fish.

You can prepare lobsters many different ways, but the simplest methods are either boiling or grilling. Obviously there are more elaborate recipes, and you may want to consult one of the many seafood cookbooks available. For us, after a day of diving, we usually want to get down to the eating, and use the simple, but excellent methods of preparation covered in this book. With these techniques, you preserve the entire subtle flavor of the lobster without an overpowering sauce or spices to distract your attention.

Prior to Cooking

If you get home and you're not quite ready to cook your lobsters, you can keep them alive for a long time by placing them in the refrigerator. We usually just place the bag of lobsters directly in the refrigerator while we clean our dive gear and take a shower. As long as you keep your lobsters cold, they will usually last for many hours this way.

Basic Boiling

Ideally, you should always cook your lobsters while they are still alive. Although many people find this distasteful, this will assure you of the best flavor. In addition, this is the safest method of preparation to avoid becoming sick due to the bacteria that begins to grow on seafood when it is allowed to sit dead for too long before it is cooked.

As previously mentioned, the simplest way to cook your lobsters is to boil them. To do this, you'll need a large pot, probably larger than anything you might normally have at home. (Well, hopefully you'll need a large pot!) Most people who are serious about lobster diving usually own at least one or more large pots of different sizes to accommodate the lobsters they catch.

Fill the pot with enough water to cover the lobsters. If you had a

If you're not ready to cook your lobster, you can always put it in the refrigerator to keep it cold.

good day, and caught more than one lobster, you may need to cook several batches, one after the other. You can reuse the water, but may need to top it up a bit between each batch of lobsters.

Some people like to add some seasonings to their water, but this is a matter of personal taste. We prefer the pure, delicate taste of the lobster itself with just the salted butter we use to dip it in.

While the pot is heating, you may want to prepare your melted butter or margarine. The easiest way to do this is to place the butter in a microwave safe cup, partially cover it with cellophane and heat it up. Don't use high heat, however, as it tends to "pop" and make a mess if you heat it too quickly.

If you don't have a microwave, place the cup in a small pot and fill the pot with water until the level of water is 3/4 of the way up the side of the cup. Place the pot on a burner on low heat and heat the water until the butter or margarine melts.

When the water is almost ready to boil in the large pot, take the lobster(s) out of the refrigerator and place them in your sink. If they have been in the refrigerator for some time they will be fairly lethargic, almost as though they are in a state of suspended animation. This doesn't mean that you don't have to be cautious when handling a lobster because they can still snap their tails unexpectedly, giving you a nasty cut.

Although you could probably toss the lobster into the pot of boiling water from a distance, this usually makes a mess and splashes scalding hot water around the kitchen. In addition, if the lobster is allowed to fall into the pot without being restrained, it will thrash its tail and throw waves of boiling water around the room. Fortunately, there is a better way to do this as explained below.

Wrap the tail of the lobster tightly and carefully in a dishtowel so that the lobster cannot flap its tail. Remove the cover from the pot and be sure that the water has reached a rapid boil.

The next step is not for the squeamish. Don a pair of oven mittens and pick up the lobster and plunge its head into the boiling water. Keep a tight grip on the lobster until you can feel that its tail has stopped any strong movements. Although the lobster will die very quickly, it will reflexively continue to struggle for a few moments.

Once the lobster has stopped most of its movement, remove the towel and drop the bug into the pot. Cover the pot immediately just in case the lobster still has any fight left in him.

Boiling is a simple but effective way to cook your lobster.

Cooking, Preparing, & Eating Lobsters

The tail of the lobster will curl under once it has been cooked. The shell will change color, too.

As soon as the water returns to a boil, remove the lid from the pot so you can keep an eye on it. As the lobster cooks, it will turn from brick red to bright red.

Keep an eye on the pot because as the lobster starts to boil, its body fluids will create a foam that frequently boils over the side of the pot. This foam is sticky and becomes difficult to clean up if allowed to dry. It will also make your kitchen quite smelly. Be prepared to turn down the heat as needed to keep the pot from boiling over. If you have too much water in the pot, you will want to scoop some of it out using a ladle to help prevent the water from boiling over.

It's difficult to tell you how long to cook your lobster because it depends on the exact size of your lobster, the size of your pot, and whether you maintain a consistent temperature. Roughly, a single legal lobster in a small pot should be fully cooked in 10-12 minutes. Large lobsters may take as long as 20 minutes or more to cook. You will need to experiment a bit with your stove until you get a feel for the exact times you need to use.

If your lobster comes out of the pot and is not fully cooked when you split it open you can always finish the job in your microwave. Clean the lobster as described in the next section before you put it in the microwave. Try to avoid overcooking the lobster or it will become tough and dry.

Some people like to brown their lobster in the broiler after boiling it. You can do this as soon as the lobster has been boiled, split and cleaned. Spread some butter on the flesh and place the lobster halves on a broiler pan with the flesh facing the flame. Slide the pan into a pre-heated broiler on the top shelf and cook until it turns a golden brown. Remove the pan from the oven and the lobster is ready to serve immediately.

How to Clean a Lobster

As soon as your lobster has finished cooking, you'll want to clean it so it's ready to eat. Wearing oven mitts, remove the pot from the stove, take it to the sink, and dump out the hot water. However, if you plan to cook another lobster, you can reuse the water and just remove the lobster using a pair of tongs.

For handling the lobster, you may want to wear a pair of heavy-duty dishwashing gloves to help avoid being burned or cut. Rinse the lobster briefly to wash off any of the foam from the cooking process.

Splitting the lobster open is best accomplished by two people working together. One person should hold the lobster down on its back on a cutting board. The tail of the lobster naturally curls under when it is cooked, and it takes a bit of effort to hold the lobster flat.

To clean the lobster you must first split it open. This job is easier if there is a second person to hold the lobster.

Clean out the sac near the head (brown), the gut and the intestinal tract that runs the length of the tail. Wash the lobster thoroughly under cold water.

To clean a smaller, raw lobster you can use a slightly different method. To remove the tail, hold the lobster down on a cutting board (or even your driveway). Be sure you are wearing gloves. Slip a small knife between the tail and the body with the blade aimed toward the head. Next, flip the bug onto its back and make another cut between the tail and the body, being careful to avoid the tail if it is still flapping. You can now pull the tail away from the body.

Twist or cut-off the tail and break off about six inches of the smaller end of one of the antennae. Insert the larger end of the cut antennae into the anal opening for about two to three inches. Give the antennae a slight twist to hook its spines into the anal tract tissue. Pull the antennae out and the entire anal tract should come with it; discard both. The tail can now be cut without any danger of anal tract contamination. You can either cook the tail or freeze it in water.

Yes, You Can Eat the Red Thing!

When you cut your lobster open, if it's a female there may be a prominent red organ on each side of the center of the body cavity. Don't throw this away! This is the "roe," or unfertilized eggs. It's quite tasty and can be eaten. However, you probably don't want to eat the white sperm packet in the male, which has the consistency of chewing gum. We can't tell you what it tastes like because we've never tried it.

On the Barbecue

If you prefer your lobsters cooked on the barbecue there are several ways to do this. You can do all of your cooking on the barbecue, or partially boil the lobster and finish the job on the grill. As with boiling, you will need to experiment a bit in order to get your cooking times right according to the type of barbecue you are using and the size of lobsters.

Most people who cook their lobsters on the grill only cook the tails this way. This is fine with a small lobster, but is wasteful of plenty of good meat if your lobster weighs more than two pounds. Of course, it's a matter of personal preference.

If you're not squeamish, you can tail your lobster by simply grabbing the tail and with a twisting, pulling motion, rip it away from the body. The more humane and refined technique, however, is to kill the lobster first by plunging it in boiling water and letting it cook for a few minutes. Remove the lobster from the pot with a pair of tongs, or just

The intestinal tract must be removed.

Rinse out the body fluids briefly using cold water. Take care not to burn your hands. You may want to wear gloves to do this.

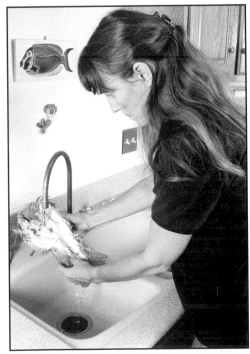

pour the water out into the sink, taking care not to burn yourself.

Once the lobster has been "tailed", split the tail with a knife to expose the meat. Remove the intestinal tract. You can cook the tail with the meat in or out of the shell, according to your preference. If you partially cooked the lobster to kill it, allow it to cool before heading for the barbecue.

If you cook the tail with the meat in the shell, start by placing the tail on the barbecue shell side down. Spread butter, paprika, and pepper on the meat and cook the tail until the shell appears burned. Once you have reached that point, flip the tail over so the meat faces the coals and continue cooking until the meat turns golden. Once the meat has turned brown, turn the tail over again and cook it for a few more minutes with the shell facing the coals. Add more butter and cook just a bit longer.

Many people prefer to cook their lobsters on the barbecue.

You can also cook the tail with the meat out of the shell. To remove the meat from the shell, stick your fork into the thickest part of the meat and lift the meat out, twisting the shell away from the meat. Marinate the meat in a mixture of melted butter, pepper, and paprika, according to your taste. Cook the meat on the barbecue until all sides are golden brown.

Jane & Skip's Lobster Dipping Recipe

Jane Dunham developed this recipe with her husband Skip, and it's a great one when you want to share your lobster with a larger group of friends. Here's their suggestion:

This recipe is not an exact science. It is something they made years ago for friends dining with them for a barbecue on a warm Santa Barbara day after Skip had a good day of lobster diving.

Cook up a large lobster (or several small ones) including the tail, body meat, and legs. Clean the lobster and place the meat in a bowl with lemon juice over it to start. Add the following ingredients:

- Cocktail sauce

- Pickle relish
- Diced scallions (green onions or chives)
- A dash or two of horseradish
- Tabasco sauce (according to taste)
- Salt and white pepper

Marinate the lobster in these ingredients for a few hours in the refrigerator. Serve this dish in a lobster bowl or on a platter along with soda crackers. Remember to use some decorative lobster napkins, because presentation is everything! Stand back when you serve this because it won't last long!

How to Eat a Whole Lobster

To get the most out of a lobster, you'll want to eat the meat in the legs, the base of the legs where they attach to the body, and the base of the antennae. There is good, tasty meat in all of these parts, and the larger the lobster, the more meat there will be.

To properly eat a whole lobster you'll need a nutcracker and a small seafood cocktail fork. These items can be purchased at most department stores and gourmet food stores.

To eat the meat in the legs, break the legs away from the body and crack them apart using the nutcracker. Eat the meat in the legs, but avoid the clear cartilage.

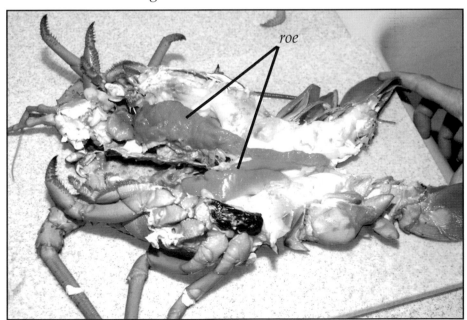

The roe of the lobster is quite tasty.

There is meat in each of the legs, a significant amount in larger lobsters. Use a nutcracker to open the legs.

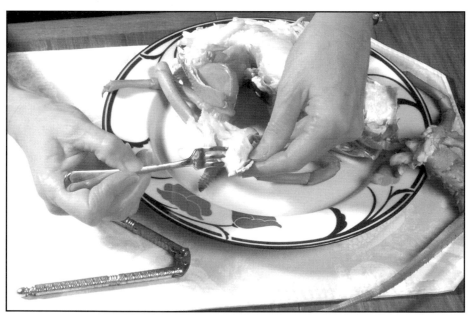

There is meat at the base of each of the legs. A small seafood fork is helpful to get this meat out of the shell.

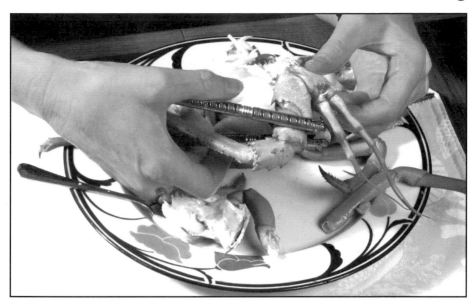

Use your nutcracker to break open the knuckle at the base of each of the antennae. There is a lot of meat here.

At the base of each leg where it attaches to the body (carapace) there is a good deal of meat. Break this portion of the legs away from the carapace and pick out the white meat. Avoid the spongy gills and cartilage.

There are good chunks of meat in the knuckles at the base of each antenna. Crack open the spiny portions of the base of each antenna and pull out the pieces of meat using your small fork. There is meat inside the body cavity, too, and although it is a different texture, it is quite flavorful.

Kristine Barsky shows off a 5 pound bug taken off the Santa Barbara coast. It takes a large pot to cook a lobster this big!

Chapter 7
Where to Hunt for Lobsters

You can find lobsters almost anyplace where there is rocky underwater habitat with a variety of invertebrates and fish. Since lobsters are scavengers they will usually be discovered where there are other animals on which they can feed.

Finding lobsters is a matter of trying different dive sites and developing an eye for the type of habitat they prefer. During the early fall, they will be found in the surf grass that it just outside the surf zone, in water as shallow as six feet deep. However, during most of the year, lobsters will be in deeper water, at depths anywhere from 15-110 feet deep. There must be holes and crevices for them to hide in where they are secure from predators. Towards late fall and into the winter look for lobsters at deeper sites.

There are different types of rocky habitat that lobsters will pick, depending on the area. Along the Santa Barbara coast and at the northern Channel Islands, lobsters will frequently be found between the shale ledges that are common to this area. However, they may also be found in areas where there are jumbled boulders or in crevices within large rocks.

There are good spots to hunt lobsters all along the coast, from San Diego to Point Conception. The locations listed are just a few of the areas that are good for lobster diving, starting from the north and working south.

Keep in mind that just because a site is good one year doesn't mean that it will be good the next. Conditions change as the sand shifts on the bottom, covering up rocks that may have made good habitat. Water temperature changes, the abundance of predators, and pollution will all affect the movement of lobsters in the marine environment.

Although the locations presented here have historically been good for lobsters, don't count on a particular spot to always produce lobsters. Try new locations whenever the opportunity presents itself. We can't guarantee that you will see lobsters at any given site, but the more ground you cover and the more spots you try, the better your chances of catching lobsters.

A Note About Marine Life Reserves

The Northern Channel Islands are located within the federally managed Channel Islands National Park. The park regulations include a number of marine life "reserves", i.e. where no game, including lobsters, may be taken. The Landing Cove at Anacapa is one such site where you can only look, but not touch.

Also located at Anacapa is a brown pelican nesting area that is closed to boat traffic and diving during much of the year. Although taking lobsters is not prohibited here, you could be ticketed for having your boat in this area.

Other areas at the Channel Islands are under study to be marked as reserves as well. There are also sites along the mainland coast that are already designated as reserves or are under consideration as reserves.

Unfortunately, there is no one place you can go to check on the legality of taking game from a specific area. You will usually need to consult several sources to ensure that you may take game at a site. For example, at the Channel Islands, both Fish and Game and the National Park Service have regulations in force. Be sure to check local laws each year, at the start of lobster season, before taking game in any area where you are uncertain of the regulations.

Marine reserves are located throughout California. Be sure to check local regulations before taking lobsters in any area.

Santa Barbara County Beach Diving
Isla Vista

Isla Vista (also known as "IV") is a student community located west of the University of California at Santa Barbara (UCSB). There is a narrow beach here that backs up to the cliffs along Del Playa Avenue. Access to the beach is down one of several stairways located between the homes along the cliff.

In the late 70s, a UCSB researcher, Jim Lindsey, did his doctoral dissertation on lobsters, and released large numbers of lobsters from the university marine lab adjacent to IV. This partially explains why the population of lobsters is good off this area even today.

During most of the year, the visibility at Isla Vista is less than 10 feet, but when there has been no rain or surf, it can improve to close to 50 feet. Isla Vista has a healthy lobster population in part because the visibility is generally poor, making diving difficult much of the year.

The surf grass close to shore along IV provides good lobster habitat in the early part of the season, and the rocky bottom offshore hides many lobsters later in the year. The maximum water depth for good hunting off Isla Vista is not over 30 feet deep, making this a good location for the novice diver.

The only drawback to IV, like most Santa Barbara coastal sites, is that there is frequently a large amount of tar floating on the surface of

Isla Vista normally has lots of kelp and offers good lobster habitat. However, visibility is usually poor at this site.

the water. The same problem exists for Carpinteria Reef and Naples Reef. If you get tar on your gear, you can remove it with vegetable oil, although any tar on a nylon coated wetsuit is almost impossible to remove completely.

Santa Barbara County Boat Diving
Naples Reef

Naples Reef is an offshore reef located just north and west of Coal Oil Point near the University of California at Santa Barbara. It is located approximately one mile from shore, with water depths of 60 feet or more surrounding it.

Naples is a good late season lobster spot after the lobsters have moved out from the shore. There are also several small rock outcroppings located inshore from Naples that can be productive when the lobsters are there.

The currents at Naples can be extremely strong and divers must use caution. Always be sure to start your dive up current from the dive boat.

Carpinteria Reef

Carpinteria Reef is a huge nearshore reef that consistently produces many lobsters. It is located a few miles east of the Santa Barbara harbor.

The shelving bottom and broken reef faces at Carpinteria provides excellent lobster habitat. Divers have worked Carpinteria Reef for many years and it still produces good quantities of lobsters.

Although this site can be accessed from shore, it is an extremely long swim and is best visited using either a kayak or a private boat. Like most offshore spots, the currents at Carpinteria can be quite strong, so always be sure to use a float line.

The visibility at Carpinteria usually averages about 10 feet, although it can get up to 50 feet. Whenever there is a "reverse current", flowing from east to west rather than the predominant west to east, the water almost always becomes extremely clear and diving is excellent.

The water depths at "Carp" Reef range from as shallow as 6 feet down to 40 feet, with most diving in the 15-25 foot range.

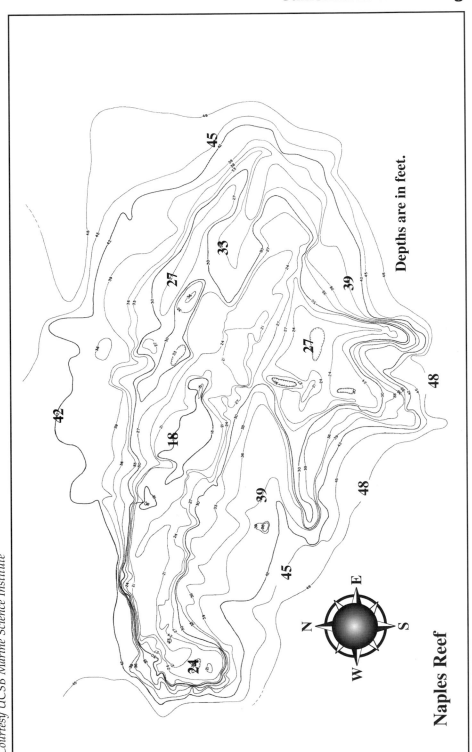

Courtesy UCSB Marine Science Institute

Depths are in feet.

Naples Reef

San Miguel Island

San Miguel Island – The Foul Area

The western end of San Miguel Island is known as the "foul area" because of the many reefs and shoals here. This is a location that requires extensive boating experience, good judgement, and caution. There are only a small number of days when it is possible to dive this site. Even on the good days, the weather can change here almost instantly, making boating extremely hazardous.

The foul area is one of the best areas at San Miguel where you can find lobsters, and the bugs that are here are typically good size. We've pulled some truly big bugs out of the foul area, including one ten-pound monster.

The bottom is shelving rock and boulders with narrow sand channels between the ledges. Visibility here is normally excellent.

The beach at Pt. Bennett hosts a large breeding colony of elephant seals and California sea lions. Don't be surprised if some of these animals swim by to check you out as you dive.

The foul area is one of the few sites along the southern California coast where great white sharks are seen with any regularity. There has been one fatal attack here and several non-fatal encounters with these animals. Caution must be exercised when diving in the foul area.

You can also find lobsters at Bay Pt. up against the island in 15 feet of water or less. This area seems to be favored primarily by males in the three to five pound range.

Santa Rosa Island

Santa Rosa Island – Talcott Shoals

Talcott Shoals is an enormous reef area located at the western end of the mainland side of Santa Rosa Island. Shelving reef comes up to within a few feet of the surface at Talcott's highest point, making good navigation a necessity.

Talcott is located several miles away from the island, and the currents here can be fierce. If you are diving from a private boat you should never leave the boat unattended while diving at Talcott. The weather at the western end of the channel can change rapidly and you must be extremely cautious.

The kelp at Talcott can be especially dense. Be sure to plan your dive well to avoid long surface swims with a heavy bag of lobsters.

The visibility at Talcott is frequently excellent, due to its distance from shore.

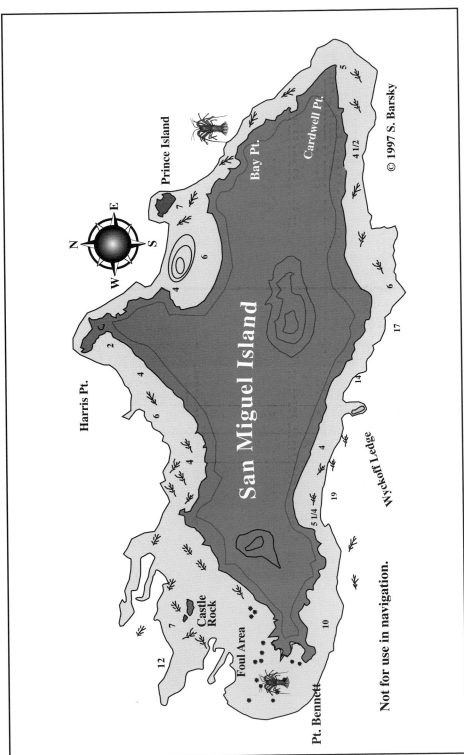

San Miguel Island

Harris Pt.

Prince Island

Bay Pt.

Cardwell Pt.

Wyckoff Ledge

Castle Rock

Foul Area

Pt. Bennett

Not for use in navigation.

© 1997 S. Barsky

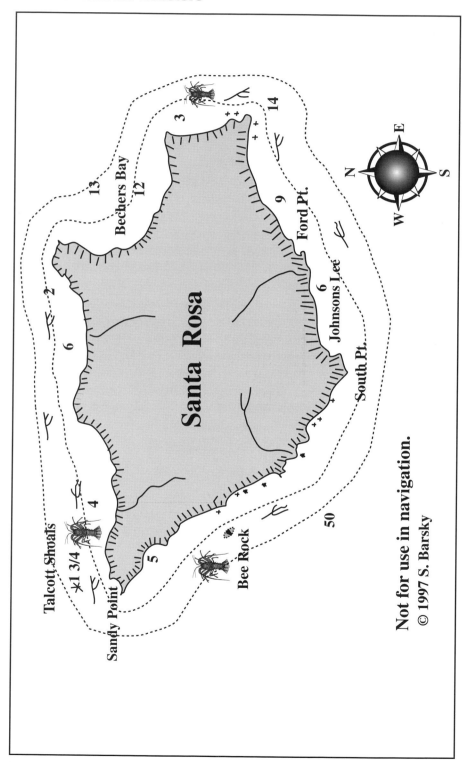

Talcott Shoals

Sandy Point

Bechers Bay

Ford Pt.

Johnsons Lee

South Pt.

Bee Rock

Santa Rosa

13

12

3

14

9

6

2

6

4

1 3/4

5

50

N E S W

Not for use in navigation.
© 1997 S. Barsky

Santa Rosa Island - East Point

The beach along this protected side of Santa Rosa is shallow and dotted with rock piles close to shore. When the swell is out of the west, this part of the island is usually calm.

This is a good site early in the season when the lobsters are in shallow water. The visibility here is usually not great, but this can be a highly productive area.

Santa Rosa Island – Bee Rock

Bee Rock is located on the southwestern side of Santa Rosa Island. It is a spectacular dive spot, whether you catch lobsters or not.

The rock is easy to find, located approximately 8 miles north and west from Johnsons Lee, or just three miles south and east of Sandy Point at the west end of Santa Rosa. It clearly sticks out of the water and there are no other exposed rocks like it on this side of the island.

Bee Rock sits not quite a mile offshore, and its exposed location can make for challenging diving when conditions are rough. This is a site that is frequently subjected to rough weather and strong currents that appear without much warning. For this reason, Bee Rock is usually considered a dive for the intermediate to advanced diver.

The kelp surrounding Bee Rock is usually fairly dense, since the waters surrounding Santa Rosa Island are almost always colder than that found further south at Anacapa or even Santa Cruz Island. With abundant kelp and dramatic relief, Bee Rock is a site that attracts a wide variety of marine life, including lobsters.

Santa Cruz Island

Santa Cruz Island - West End

The north side of the west end of Santa Cruz Island is a good lobster area with numerous holes and crevices where lobsters can be found. Almost any likely looking cove will hold some lobsters.

The whole area from Fry's Harbor to the West end of the island can be extremely productive at the right time of year. The bottom at this end of the island falls off sharply into deep water. There are sheer walls sloping down from the island with large boulders and sand at their base.

Most of the coves at this end of Santa Cruz are small and you must anchor carefully. Keep in mind that if you venture outside the coves the currents can be quite strong.

Santa Cruz Island - Yellowbanks

The Yellowbanks area at the eastern end of Santa Cruz lies offshore

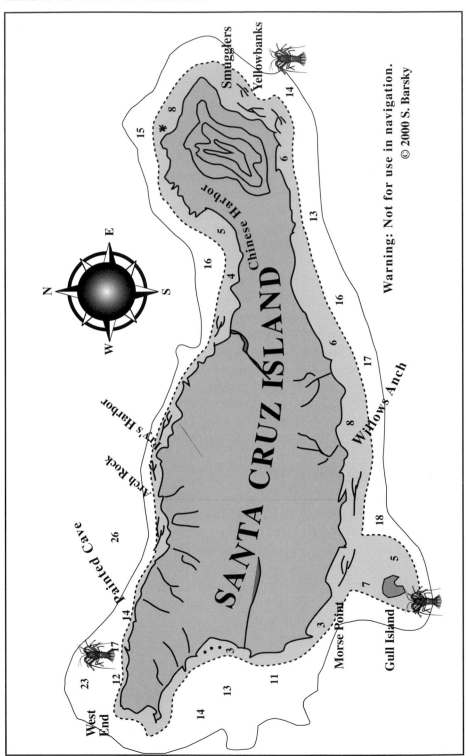

Smugglers

Yellowbanks

15

8

*

6

14

Chinese Harbor

5

13

16

4

16

6

17

Willows Anch

8

18

5

7

Gull Island

3

Morse Point

11

13

14

3

14

23

17

12

West End

26

Arch Rock

Fry's Harbor

Painted Cave

SANTA CRUZ ISLAND

N E S W

Warning: Not for use in navigation.

© 2000 S. Barsky

from the island with water depths ranging from 40-80 feet deep. Scattered rocks and sections of low reef here provide good habitat for lobsters.

If you are diving from a small boat, you will need a fathometer to help pick out good sections of reef. The kelp here can be quite thick at times, so be sure to plan your dive carefully to avoid a difficult surface swim. Yellowbanks also has some of the strongest currents at the island, and you must always start your dive upcurrent.

Santa Cruz Island – Gull Island

Gull Island is located approximately one mile from shore, off the seaward side of Santa Cruz Island and a mile and a half southeast of Morse Point. Like Bee Rock at Santa Rosa, Gull Island is exposed to strong currents that can sweep a diver away quickly. Always be sure to carry both a visual and audible signaling device when diving sites like these.

The terrain around Gull Island is scattered rocks and boulders that rise to the surface and drop off to depths of 70 feet or more. The bottom is covered with purple coral, gorgonians, and numerous invertebrates. This is good lobster habitat.

Anacapa Island

Anacapa is the smallest of the Northern Channel Islands and has a limited number of places where you can hunt for lobsters. There is no good anchorage for an overnight stay at this island, so most visitors are on day trips only. The closest island anchorage is at Smugglers Cove at Santa Cruz Island, several miles north and west.

Anacapa Island - Coral Reef

Coral Reef, on the south side of the island, sits offshore approximately a mile from the island. It rises to within 30 feet of the surface and drops off to depths in excess of 80 feet on the outside.

Coral Reef usually has good visibility. It is a beautiful spot to dive and lobsters can be found here, primarily later in the season.

Coral Reef is exposed to strong currents and caution must be exercised at this site.

Anacapa Island - West End, South Side

The west end of the island is an area with a good lobster population, although the bottom here is difficult to work. Large jumbled boulders provide plenty of hiding spaces for lobsters, making it diffi-

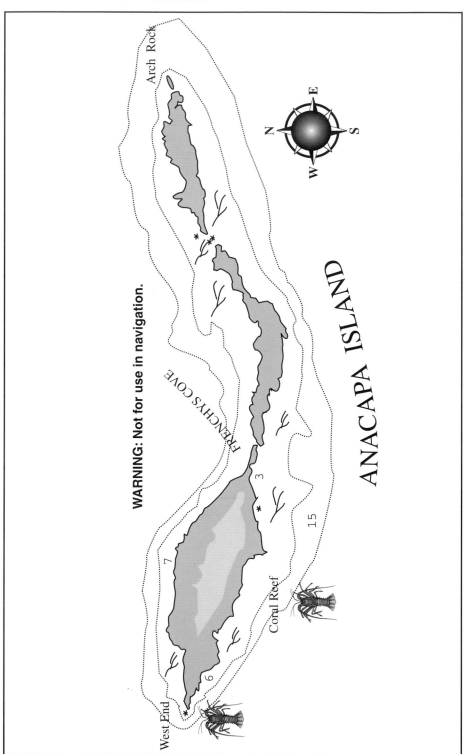

Divers Jeff James and Dave Anderson show off the results of a good day at the Channel Islands. There are three limits of lobster in this photo, and the third limit was taken by the photographer, Skip Dunham.(© Skip Dunham. All rights reserved.)

cult to grab them. The area within a mile of the west end of the island is particularly good for hunting.

Santa Barbara Island

Santa Barbara Island is the most southern island in Channel Islands National Park. It is one of the smaller islands and the most remote in the group.

Santa Barbara Island usually has excellent visibility as it is more remote and further south than the Northern Channel Islands. The only anchorage here is on the eastern side of the island. The visibility at Santa Barbara, like Catalina, San Clemente, and San Nicolas tends to be better than the visibility at the northern islands because the water is usually warmer.

Santa Barbara Island - Sutil Island

The bottom surrounding Sutil Island provides some good lobster habitat. The marine growth here is lush and there are many crevices and cracks where lobsters can hide.

The bottom at Sutil Island tends to fall away rather rapidly on the southeastern side. There are large boulders here and good lobster habitat.

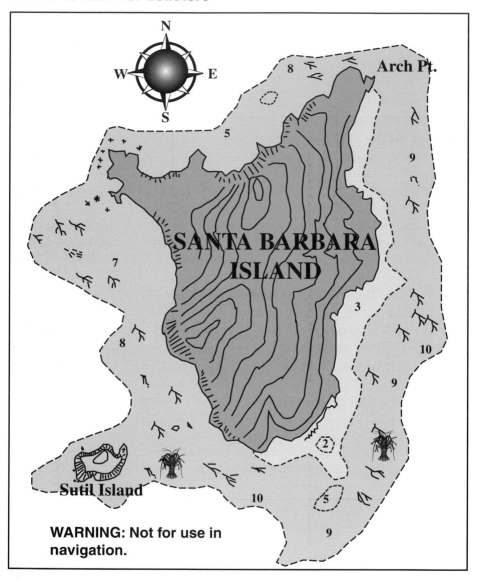

Santa Barbara Island
Southeastern Side

The southeastern side of Santa Barbara Island is a spectacular area with dramatic reef. There are massive towering reefs here with sand channels that run between them. It is a fabulous diving area and a good spot for lobsters. There is a restriction here that lobsters may not be taken in waters shallower than 20 feet deep. This area is part of the Santa Barbara Island Ecological Reserve.

Another good spot at Santa Barbara Island is the Arch.

Malibu
Paradise Cove
Located near Pt. Dume, Paradise Cove boasts a shelving reef in 30-60 feet of water. This can be a good lobster spot from the middle of the season to late in the year.

Santa Catalina Island
Santa Catalina Island (or just "Catalina" as most people call it) remains the most popular diving destination in California, and yet it remains a good spot to hunt for lobsters. As the closest island to Los Angeles, Catalina receives a large number of visitors on a daily basis.

Divers should be especially careful to avoid any violation of Fish and Game laws while diving at Catalina. The court on Catalina has been known to order diver's equipment forfeited in addition to levying the maximum fines allowable by law.

There are several closure areas at Catalina where no game may be taken. These include Big Fisherman Cove (the site of the USC Marine laboratory) and the Lover's Cove Reserve. The Lover's Cove Reserve near the city of Avalon, starts at the southeasterly corner of the Cabrillo Wharf and extends in a line seaward, perpendicular to the wharf to a point 100 yards from the mean tide line. It continues through Lover's Cove, around Abalone Point, and extends to a point 430 feet east of Abalone Point, commonly known as Ring Rock, returning to shore on a line perpendicular to the Pebble Beach Road.

Another invertebrate closure exists from the high tide mark to 1000 feet beyond the low tide mark along the lee side of the island between Lion Head Point and Arrow Point.

Catalina Island – Isthmus Reef
Isthmus Reef is a large tabletop reef located on the mainland side at the narrowest point of the island. This area receives heavy boat traffic and divers must be extremely cautious when diving here.

Catalina Island – Eagle Reef
Eagle Reef is one of the best dive sites at Catalina and a good place for lobsters, particularly at night. The underwater terrain here is quite varied, with ledges and overhangs where lobsters can hide. The kelp at Eagle Reef can be thick, and the habitat is excellent for a variety of species. In several places the reef comes quite close to the surface. Boat operators must use caution when navigating close to the reef.

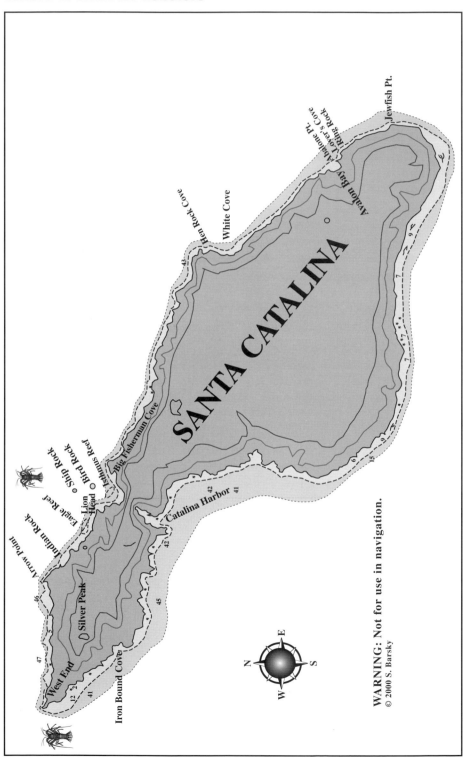

SANTA CATALINA

Jewfish Pt.

Bird Rock Cove
Lover's Cove
Abalone Pt.
Avalon Bay

White Cove

Hen Rock Cove

Big Fisherman Cove

Isthmus Reef
Bird Rock
Ship Rock
Lion Head
Eagle Reef
Indian Rock
Arrow Point

Silver Peak

West End

Iron Bound Cove

Catalina Harbor

WARNING: Not for use in navigation.
© 2000 S. Barsky

N E S W

Catalina Island – West End

The western end of the island is good for lobsters on both the mainland and ocean sides. Steep rocks and caves dot this area making for good lobster diving. Beware of strong currents at the tip of the island.

Other spots where there is good lobster diving at Catalina include the Hen Rock Cove area and Arrow Point.

Los Angeles County
Santa Monica Bay Artificial Reefs

In 1961 the Department of Fish and Game built three "replication" reefs in Santa Monica Bay to evaluate automobile bodies, concrete fish shelters (made from modified concrete dock floats) and quarry rock as materials for artificial reefs. The automobile bodies have long since rusted away, and the Department has cooperated with others to build more reefs, so there are now eight quarry rock/concrete rubble reefs scattered from Malibu to Redondo Beach. You'll need a boat to get to the reefs, located in areas of great expanses of sand bottom in Santa Monica Bay. At certain times of the year, often in mid-October to mid-November, lobsters appear on the reefs "overnight as if by magic."

We have noted earlier that lobsters have been reported to move onshore-offshore and to have been seen in "bull rings" in sandy habitat. Their brief appearance at these reefs year after year is the best circumstantial evidence for long-distance movement in California spiny lobster. The water depths at the reefs varies from 28 to 72 feet, dependent on which reef you are diving.

Redondo Beach – King Harbor Breakwater

The outside of the King Harbor breakwater at Redondo Beach has always been a productive spot for lobster diving, although the visibility is usually poor. Diving along breakwaters is usually best at night, as the lobsters are more accessible.

Another good site in the Redondo area is the reef off Topaz Street.

Los Angeles County – Palos Verdes

The Palos Verdes Peninsula has always been a good lobster area, but you must have a small boat to access it. Almost anywhere in Palos Verdes has potential at the right time of the year. One of the best locations is the area surrounding the wreck of the *Dominator*. Another good spot is Malaga Cove.

Breakwaters, like this one at Redondo Beach, are good lobster habitat, but visibility is usually poor and you must be cautious regarding boat traffic.

Palos Verdes – *The Dominator*

The *Dominator* was a Greek freighter that ran aground on March 13, 1961 near Rocky Point. She broke up despite several attempts at salvage. Today the *Dominator* is in pieces, but the wreckage makes for a great lobster dive when conditions are good.

The danger in diving the *Dominator* is that this is an exposed site that is subject to large swells. Many jagged and sharp pieces of metal remain at the site.

The kelp at the wreck can be quite thick, but the lush bottom is part of what makes this a good spot to search for lobsters. Launch your boat at either Redondo Harbor or San Pedro to dive the *Dominator*.

San Pedro - White's Point to Point Fermin

This several mile long stretch of relatively accessible coast line is shallow water ledges and boulders, out to depths of 20 - 25 feet if diving from shore, or out to 50 - 60 feet if you are on a boat. Look for public park access along Paseo del Mar, or drive all the way down to the water's edge at the Royal Palms - White's Point park.

Los Angeles/Long Beach Breakwater

The outside of the Los Angeles/Long Beach breakwater has long been a favorite spot for lobster divers. The visibility here tends to be

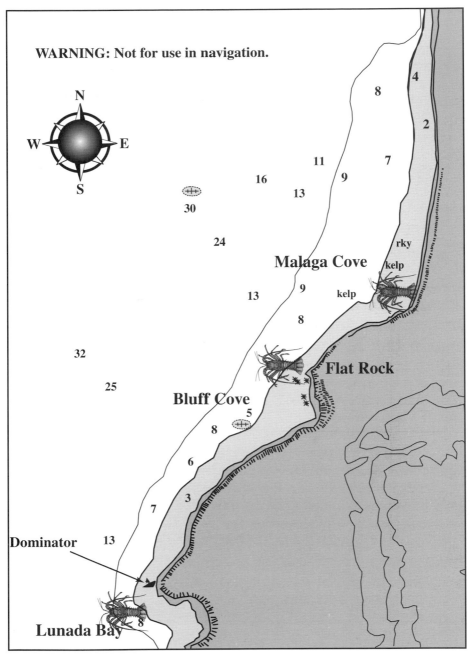

WARNING: Not for use in navigation.

N
W   E
S

4

8

2

11   7

16   9

13

30

24

Malaga Cove

rky

kelp

9   kelp

13

8

32

13   9

kelp

8

25

Flat Rock

Bluff Cove

5

8

6

3

7

Dominator   13

Lunada Bay   8

The Palos Verdes Peninsula has numerous spots to dive. For most sites, you will need a boat, as there is limited shore access.

Where to Hunt for Lobsters

The rugged coast along the Palos Verdes peninsula continues to be a popular lobster diving area.

Angel's Gate lighthouse

The Los Angeles/Long Beach breakwater is enormous. This is only a small portion of the breakwater.

Crystal Cove State Park encompasses a large section of the coast.

poor, but the jumbled rock face on the outside of the breakwater provides some excellent lobster habitat. This is a popular night diving spot.

Boat traffic on the outside of the breakwater is always heavy and divers must use caution when diving here. Be sure to fly a diver's flag and if you are night diving be sure your boat is properly lit.

Laguna Beach

Much of the area in Laguna Beach is an ecological reserve where no game may be taken. Most sites are well posted with signs, but if you are new to the area it is always wise to stop at one of the local dive stores to check the latest local regulations.

Laguna Beach – Crystal Cove
(formerly known as Scotchman's Cove/Horse Pastures)

Crystal Cove is a large cove at the northern end of Laguna Beach. High cliffs border the cove and it is a long hike down to the beach. Most people prefer to dive this site from a boat, although shore diving is possible.

There are numerous rocks, boulders, and crevices where lobsters can hide in the water off Crystal Cove. Deeper reefs lie offshore in waters down to 70 feet in depth.

There are numerous rocks in shallow water at Moss Cove. Beach entries must be made with care.

Laguna Beach - Moss Cove

Moss Cove is an excellent dive site and a popular spot to dive for lobsters. There is a steep stairway to the narrow but picturesque beach here. Parking is extremely limited so you must arrive at the beach early. This is generally considered to be an advanced dive site, due to the extremely rocky bottom that can make entry and exit difficult.

Excellent rocky habitat makes Moss Cove a good spot for lobsters.

San Nicholas Island

Numerous large lobsters have been taken at San Nicholas Island over the years, although the large bugs there have become increasingly rare. It is the most isolated and remote of the islands off southern California. Controlled by the Navy, diving here is often restricted.

San Nicholas Island – The Boiler

This spot is located approximately two miles from the western tip of the island. This spot is known for strong currents and large lobsters. It is not for the novice diver.

San Nicholas Island - Seven Fathom Reef

This reef starts at fifty feet. Why this spot is called Seven Fathom Reef is a bit obscure, since a fathom is six feet. However, this location

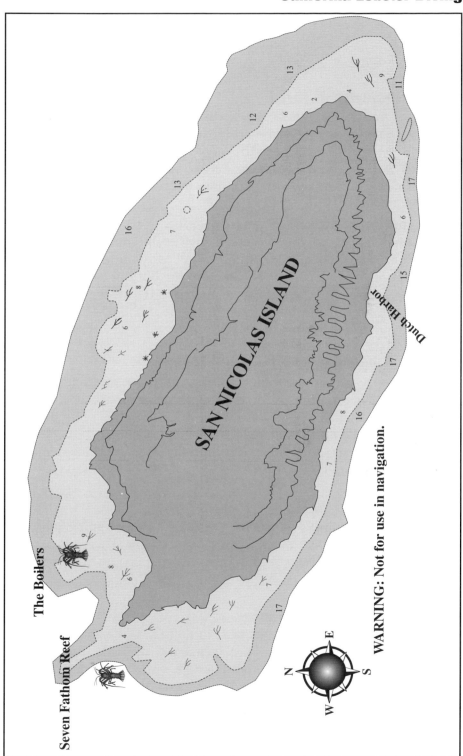

SAN NICOLAS ISLAND

The Boilers

Seven Fathom Reef

Dutch Harbor

WARNING: Not for use in navigation.

presents some excellent terrain with shelves and terraces where lobsters can hide. It's also a good spot for photos with (usually) thick kelp. The currents here can be strong.

San Clemente Island

San Clemente Island is the furthest south of the islands off California. Portions of the island are closed to civilian boat activity due to Navy operations here. Check the most recent marine charts and the Notice to Mariners on a regular basis to be sure you are not entering a restricted area. Naval target practice may be hazardous to your health!

San Clemente Island - Pyramid Cove

Pyramid Cove is a wide, protected cove at the southern end of San Clemente Island. The kelp growth here is usually quite dense and the area has numerous reefs that rise up from the bottom to within a few feet of the surface. At the outside of the cove the water drops off to depths in excess of 70 feet, but most diving is in the 40-60 foot range. There are numerous lobsters here, but most tend to be small.

San Clemente Island - Pyramid Head

Pyramid Head is the point at the southeastern end of San Clemente. It is an exciting area to dive, with sheer rock faces that drop off into deep water. The shallow areas surrounding this point provide many nooks and crannies where lobsters can hole up.

Other diving spots that have traditionally been good lobster spots include Northwest Harbor, China Point, and Mail Point.

San Diego/La Jolla

The San Diego area is the center of the California spiny lobster's range and is an excellent place to hunt for lobsters. There are several good beach diving spots in the La Jolla area that can be quite productive.

La Jolla - Boomer's Beach

This is an advanced dive site next to La Jolla Cove, just outside of the reserve. The beach entry here is usually difficult due to large waves. There are big boulders and ledges providing many hiding places for lobsters. The kelp growth here can also be heavy making good underwater navigation essential. Diving depths range from 20-45 feet and visibility usually ranges from 15-20 feet.

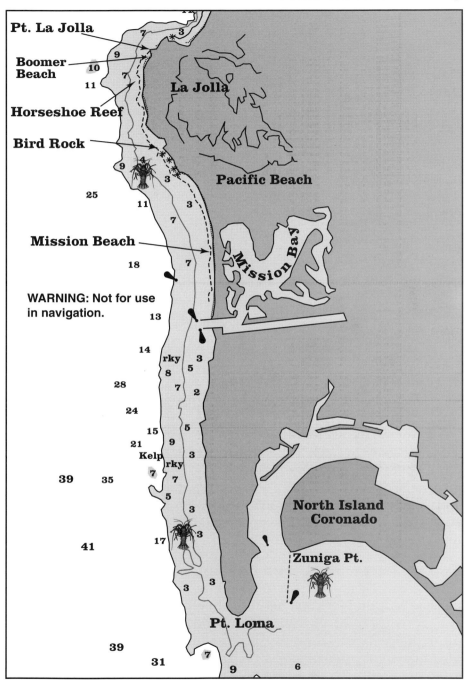

Pt. La Jolla

Boomer
Beach

Horseshoe Reef

Bird Rock

La Jolla

Pacific Beach

Mission Beach

WARNING: Not for use
in navigation.

Mission Bay

rky

Kelp

rky

North Island
Coronado

Zuniga Pt.

Pt. Loma

La Jolla – Horseshoe Reef

Deep underwater ledges at Horseshoe Reef allow lobsters to remain beyond the grasp of divers during the day, but make this one of the better night diving spots in the area. The beach here is almost all rock with surf grass just in the surf line and slightly beyond. Care must be taken during your entry to avoid slipping and falling.

At night, the lobsters can often be found on top of the ledges, making for an easy grab. You can "jump" from ledge to ledge following the sand channels between each section of the reef.

La Jolla - Bird Rock

Located at the southern end of La Jolla, the Bird Rock area covers almost a mile and a half of underwater terrain. The diving here starts in water as shallow as five feet deep and extends out to 50 feet of water. There are steps at the north side of the cove leading down to the pebble-covered beach.

Visibility at Bird Rock is usually poor, requiring divers to use the Braille method of diving (hands stretched out in front of you while moving slowly) to avoid running into rocks. However, the low visibility keeps most divers away and allows the lobsters to hide. In most cases, you won't see the lobsters until you are right on top of them.

San Diego - Point Loma

From the Mission Bay jetty all the way down to the tip of Point Loma, and for a couple of miles beyond, from the shore out to depths of about 80 feet there is superb lobster habitat. Surf grass beds, low relief mudstone shelves, rock out crops, great giant kelp beds and even ship wreckage - it's all here.

Between La Jolla and Point Loma, it is not unusual for the commercial fishery to catch 25 percent of the statewide season total from this area. Even though most regular San Diego area divers have their favorite spots, you can jump in almost anywhere along Point Loma, and as noted earlier, if you don't see lobsters fairly quickly, then either keep swimming or move the boat and dive again, until you do find them.

Zuniga Jetty - San Diego Bay Entrance

The San Diego Port District prohibits recreational diving inside Ballast Point, and for good reason with all the vessel traffic in the Bay. However, just south of Ballast Point, and marking the eastern side of the entrance to San Diego Bay, parallel to Point Loma is Zuniga Jetty. This man-made quarry rock structure is diveable only by boat, as it extends from the North Island Naval Base shore line for over a mile, with water depths of from 6 to about 30 feet, and it is some of the best lobster habitat in California. It's so good that you won't come close to catching a lobster here in the daytime, but at night, it's a different story.

The lobsters come out of their deep, deep holes to forage on the top of the jetty and the surrounding surf grass beds. It is best at the start of the season, but there are some lobsters to catch here all the way up to the closing Wednesday in March. Be sure to check the tide tables and watch for the water flow, as it can be quite strong at times. A compass is also a necessity, so you can make your dive oriented along the long axis of the jetty, but still be able to swing out on to the sand and safely make your way back without having to surface in an area of lots of boat traffic. The Jetty is also a popular place for hoop-netters to fish for lobster, so be courteous and exercise caution when you see other boats around.

Imperial Beach Cobble Beds

This is another area reachable only by boat, and it's rather nebulous in its definition. You'll want to go below the Imperial Beach Pier, but stay well north above the mouth of the Tiajuana River. The cobble beds extend into about 15 feet of water and out to 50 - 60 feet. This is one of the strangest places in California to dive for lobsters.

Do not dive this area after periods of heavy rain as the pollution levels can be extremely high. If in doubt, check with the health department or lifeguards regarding whether the site is safe for diving.

As the name implies, the bottom consists of cobbles, or rocks from the size of your fist up to a couple of feet in diameter, all in a firm sand sea floor. Many times, there are no lobster here, but on those special occasions, when they seem to march through the area, they have "no place to hide, nowhere to go" and present you with the easiest daytime lobster grabbing you can imagine. It's a place to swim fast and cover lots of territory, which is easy to do if the visibility is more than 10 - 15 feet, but of course it may not be that good. Those days you'll wonder why you didn't stay up at Point Loma. But on that special day, you'll know why you came all the way down to within a few miles of the international boundary, and you'll be glad you did.

About the Authors

Kristine Barsky

Kristine Barsky (*née* Henderson) was always a water person, who learned to swim early, and swam competitively when she was in grade school. She started scuba diving when she was in college in 1972, and became a NAUI assistant instructor in 1985.

Kristine is a Humboldt State University graduate with a degree in Zoology. She also has an AA in Wildlife Law and Conservation. She started a Master's degree, but the lure of a job in the field, left her advanced degree unfinished. She worked a variety of jobs, some in biology, and others more practical, before landing a permanent job with the California Dept. of Fish and Game in 1979. She was hired as a marine biologist who could dive.

Kristine went through Fish and Game's diving certification program six months after she joined the Department and became an official Department diver. She is still a member of the Department"s diving program, and goes through an annual diving recertification course every year.

Her first two years with Fish and Game were spent doing surveys above and below the surface off the northern coast of Santa Barbara County. A transfer to Long Beach put her on the nearshore invertebrate project for seven years. On that project she sometimes logged over 200 dives a year counting abalone and sea urchins on the bottom along the coast and off most of California's offshore islands. She also spent a lot of time planting juvenile abalones of all sizes.

Kristine returned to Santa Barbara in 1988 when she married Steve and became Kristine Barsky. She became the Department's Unit manager for marine recreational and commercial fisheries, for the next 12 years. As the Department's liaison in the area, she also interacted with local mariculturists, government agencies, and the public. At the end of 1999, she took a position as the Department's marine invertebrate specialist.

Kristine has authored scientific papers and is a regular speaker at scientific conferences. She also has given many presentations at sport diving programs.

Steve and Kristine dive the Channel Islands on a regular basis and travel internationally whenever they get the opportunity. She enjoys modeling for Steve, and being out on the ocean. Steve, the naturalist,

Kristine Barsky is a professional marine biologist.

and Kristine, the biologist, are always checking out the marine life during their adventures underwater. She hopes that this book will not only make you a successful hunter, but give you an appreciation and love for one of the fascinating creatures that live beneath the sea.

Steven M. Barsky

Steve Barsky started diving in 1965 in Los Angeles County, and became a NAUI instructor in 1970. His first employment in the industry was with a dive store in Los Angeles and he went on to work for almost 10 years in the retail dive store environment.

Steve attended the University of California at Santa Barbara, where he earned a Masters Degree in 1976 in Human Factors Engineering. This has greatly helped in his thorough understanding of diving equipment design and use. His master's thesis was one of the first to deal with the use of underwater video systems in commercial diving. His work was a pioneering effort at the time (1976) and was used by the Navy in developing applications for underwater video systems.

His background includes being a commercial diver, working in the offshore oil industry in the North Sea, Gulf of Mexico, and South America. He worked as both an air diving supervisor and a mixed gas saturation diver, making working dives down to 580'.

About the Authors

Steve Barsky is a full-time consultant and photographer for the diving industry.

In 1978, Barsky joined the staff of the Florida PADI College in Jacksonville, Florida. As Training Director, Barsky was responsible for open water training and screening applicants for admission into the College. This program was one of the first private extended instructor training programs in the country, after which all current programs of this type are modeled.

Barsky was marketing manager for Viking America, Inc., an international manufacturer of dry suits. He also served in a similar position at Diving Systems International (DSI), the world's leading manufacturer of commercial diving helmets. At DSI, Barsky worked very closely with Bev Morgan, a diving pioneer.

Steve is an accomplished underwater photographer. His photos have been used in numerous magazine articles, catalogs, advertising, training programs, and textbooks.

A prolific writer, Barsky's work has been published in *Alert Diver, Sea Technology, The Los Angeles Times, Underwater USA, Skin Diver, Offshore Magazine, Emergency, Fire Engineering, Dive Training Magazine, Searchlines, Sources, Undersea Biomedical Reports, Santa Barbara Magazine, Selling Scuba, Scuba Times, Underwater Magazine,* and many other publications. He is the author of the *Dry Suit Diving Manual, Diving in High-Risk Environments, Spearfishing for Skin and Scuba Divers, Small Boat Diving, Diving with the EXO-26 Full Face Mask, Diving with the Divator MK II Full Face Mask*, and a joint author with Dick Long and Bob Stinton of *Dry Suit Diving: A Guide to Diving Dry*. He is also a joint author of *Careers in Diving*, with his wife, Kristine and Ronnie Damico. Steve has taught numerous workshops on contaminated water diving, dry suits, small boat diving, spearfishing, and other diving topics. *The Simple Guide to Rebreather Diving* was written by Steve along with Mark Thurlow and Mike Ward.

In 1989 Steve formed Marine Marketing and Consulting, based in Santa Barbara, California. The company provides market research, marketing plans, consulting, newsletters, promotional articles, technical manuals, and other services for the diving and ocean industry. He has consulted to Dräger, AquaLung/U.S. Divers Co., Inc., Zeagle Systems, Inc., Diving Unlimited Intnl., Diving Systems Intnl., DAN, NAUI, and numerous other companies. He also investigates diving accidents and serves as an expert witness in dive accident litigation.

In 1999, Steve and his wife Kristine formed Hammerhead Press to publish high quality diving books. Hammerhead Press is a subsidiary of the Carcharodon Corporation.

Steve is an instructor with NAUI and PADI, as well as a TDI rebreather diving instructor for the Dräger semi-closed circuit system.

Bibliography

Bodkin, J. L. and Brown, L. 1992. *Molt frequency and size-class distribution in the California spiny lobster (Panulirus interruptus) as indicated by beach-cast carapaces at San Nicolas Island, California.* Vol. 78, No. 4, p 136-144.

Duffy, J. M. 1973. *The status of the California spiny lobster resource.* Calif. Dept. Fish & Game, Marine Resources Technical Rept. 10. 15 pp.

Engle, J.M. 1979. *The ecology and growth of juvenile California spiny lobster, Panulirus interruptus (Randall).* Sea Grant Dissertation Series, USCSC-TD-03-79. 298 pp.

Jensen, G.C. 1995. *Pacific coast crabs and shrimps.* Sea Challengers, Monterey, CA. 87 pp.

Leet, W.S., Dewees, C.M., and C.W. Haugen, eds. 1992. *California's living marine resources and their utilization.* Sea Grant Extension Publication, UCSGEP-92-12. 257 pp.

Lindberg, R.G. 1955 *Growth, population dynamics, and field behavior in the spiny lobster, Panulirus interruptus (Randall).* University of California Publication Zoology, Vol. 59, No. 6, p. 158-231.

Lindsey, J. 1976. *Contact chemoreceptor mechanisms in the California rock lobster, Panulirus interrruptus (Randall).* A Dissertation. U.C. Santa Barbara, 159 pp.

Mitchell, C.T., C.H. Turner, and A.R. Strachan. 1969 *Observations on the biology and behavior of the California spiny lobster, Panulirus interruptus (Randall).* Calif. Fish and Game, Vol. 55, p. 121-131.

Odemar, M.W., R.R. Bell, C.W. Haugen, and R.A. Hardy. 1975. *Report on California spiny lobster, Panulirus interruptus (Randall) research with recommendations for management.* Calif. Fish and Game Operations Resources Branch. 98 pp. (Special Publication).

Index

Index

Index

Index